THE
MAKING OF AMERICA
SERIES

WARWICK

A CITY AT THE CROSSROADS

This handsome farmhouse and barn were part of the Hill Farm in 1870. During times of low production at the mill, selected workers would help out with the chores and tasks out at the farm. (Courtesy Raymond West Collection.)

THE
MAKING OF AMERICA
SERIES

WARWICK
A CITY AT THE CROSSROADS

DONALD A. D'AMATO

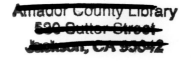

ARCADIA

Copyright © 2001 by Donald A. D'Amato.
ISBN 0-7385-2369-0

Published by Arcadia Publishing,
an imprint of Tempus Publishing, Inc.
2 Cumberland Street
Charleston, SC 29401

Printed in Great Britain.

Library of Congress Catalog Card Number: 2001094272

For all general information contact Arcadia Publishing at:
Telephone 843-853-2070
Fax 843-853-0044
E-Mail sales@arcadiapublishing.com

For customer service and orders:
Toll-Free 1-888-313-2665

Visit us on the Internet at http://www.arcadiapublishing.com

To those who follow his column in the *Warwick Beacon* every Thursday, author Don D'Amato is the man who has made the history of Warwick and Rhode Island come to life. Many years of teaching Rhode Island history in the Warwick School System and at the Community College of Rhode Island have increased his knowledge and interest in the material in this book.

In 1985, Don D'Amato was appointed as Warwick's official city historian, a position he continues to hold today. His many books include *Warwick's 350-Year Heritage*, *Coventry Celebration*, *General James M. Varnum*, and *Warwick Firefighters*. He has also written a history of Johnson & Wales University called *A Dream that Became a Reality* and a number for the *Images of America* series, which include *Warwick*, *Pawtuxet*, and *Block Island*.

CONTENTS

FOREWORD

As a lifelong resident of the city of Warwick and a student of history, I am pleased to write this foreword to Don D'Amato's newest look at the history of the city.

The 359 years that have passed since our humble beginnings as the settlement of Shawomet have been an exciting testament to the resiliency of the human spirit, the compassion and patience of our citizenry, and the ethics and value of the institutions of our government.

From the time that Samuel Gorton led us from the wilderness and into the light of a new and glorious community, the people of Warwick have fully understood that the combination of our people and the scenic beauty of our city are truly our best assets.

This newest installment of Warwick's history from Don D'Amato highlights and showcases the men, women, and children that have grown Warwick into Rhode Island's second largest city, the crossroads of southern New England, and the shining gem that we call home.

I applaud all that have gone before us and have toiled to make the city of Warwick an exciting, vibrant, and viable part of the state of Rhode Island.

—Scott Avedisian
Mayor of Warwick
2001

Acknowledgments

The truth of the words of the poet John Donne, "No man is an island entire of itself . . .," never seemed as clear to me as when writing about the history of Warwick. When I first began writing articles for the *Warwick Beacon* in 1983, John Howell told me my greatest pleasure would derive from the people I would meet and work with.

Since that time, I have been amazed by the generosity, knowledge, and friendship I have received from so many excellent local historians. From the very beginning, Henry A.L. Brown has shared his large historical collection, and even more importantly, he has been a true friend. I have also been helped and encouraged by colleagues Donald Brown, Thomas E. Greene, and Richard Siembab, and by Mayors Flaherty, Donovan, Chafee, and Avedisian.

Along with the help of these and many other friends, I have been blessed with Gary Melino's photographic skill, Maxwell May's artistic ability, and especially by my wife Jean's multi-talented contributions. Jean has assisted in every phase of the research and writing. Most of all, she has read the manuscript, correcting, commenting, and improving at every turn. Without Jean, no book would have been possible.

I am truly grateful.

—Don D'Amato

INTRODUCTION

In 1931, the town of Warwick, reeling from the devastating impact of the stock market crash of 1929 and seeing its mill village economy in serious collapse, tried desperately for a solution. The political leaders at the time felt the answer might be found in getting the village chartered as a city.

Like many other New England towns, the increase in population in Warwick made the town meeting form of government unwieldy and inefficient. By 1931, Warwick's population exceeded 23,000, which included approximately 13,000 qualified voters. All monies to conduct town services had to be appropriated by the financial town meetings. As there were over 9,000 qualified taxpayers, the town meeting had become too large to be practical. No party had control over the town meeting and the five-man town council found itself with a number of financial difficulties. They believed that a city government, with a mayor and council, would be much more effective.

After two unsuccessful bids to get a charter, a movement led by Harold P. Whyte, president of the Warwick Chamber of Commerce, was successful in winning support to change the government. The City Charter was accepted on April 21, 1931, and an election was called in November 1932, with the first mayor and city council to assume office in March 1933.

The first mayor elected was Pierce Brereton, who had been city solicitor from 1926 to 1932. He was the front runner in the campaign and won easily. In 1932, Warwick was one of the few cities in the state to vote Republican, selecting Brereton and a predominately Republican city council.

Warwick was inhabited, of course, long before it became a city. By the time the first English settlers came to the area, the Narragansett Indians had established a definite pattern of civilization and fully utilized and managed the forests and the bay. The large influx of Europeans during the seventeenth and eighteenth centuries changed the land from a heavily forested area to one of intense farming, and a number of political changes occurred due to their different cultural traditions and beliefs.

The original purchase made by Samuel Gorton covered approximately 107 square miles. In 1741, the western section was partitioned off to create the town of Coventry, as transportation was too difficult to make one political entity feasible. During the nineteenth century, the land and the rivers took on a new significance as industry came into the area. Most of the heavy industry occurred in the western section, bringing not

Warwick's beautifully restored City Hall welcomes visitors to the "City at the Crossroads."

only new wealth, but also changing the emphasis and the priorities of use of the land and of the Pawtuxet River. To satisfy the textile manufacturers, laws were enacted to allow for the needs of the industry. In time, the agricultural eastern section and the industrialized west differed so greatly that, in 1913, another separation was called for. At this point, West Warwick, comprising about 13 square miles, was created.

By the time it became a city in 1931, Warwick was primarily an agricultural community, and the tax base was on land value. Over 10,204 acres were devoted to farming. In Warwick and West Warwick, there were 221 farms. Warwick had over 7,000 apple trees, 1,600 peach trees, and 5,600 grapevines. Its cows produced 470,000 gallons of milk, and a thriving dairy business resulted. The larger farms in the town prospered as the growing population of greater Providence provided a good market for Warwick's fruits, vegetables, and dairy products.

Brereton and the Republican-dominated nine-man council had campaigned on the promise of reducing taxes, and their budget reflected the pledge since the tax rate was reduced from $2.40 to $2.35. Unfortunately, this resulted in a reduction of salaries of all city employees.

The airport was in its infancy, and there was no Route I-95 or I-295. There were no malls or large retail stores. Indeed, critics of Warwick's claim to be regarded as a city pointed out that one couldn't even buy a suit of clothes in Warwick.

All this has changed dramatically. The period of rapid growth came after World War II, when the city grew at an unprecedented rate. The demand for housing and the development of a modern system of highways began to transform the once agricultural community into its present status. Changes in the use of the land brought about a

9

By the early twentieth century, Apponaug was the hub of Warwick's economic and political life. Automobile traffic was already heavy near the Four Corners. (Courtesy Dorothy Mayor Collection.)

transition in the population as well. Over the centuries, people from all continents and races have called Warwick home—from early Paleo-American hunters to Narragansett Indians in the prehistoric period, to English immigrants in the seventeenth and eighteenth centuries, to Irish, French-Canadian, Italian, Swedish, Polish, and other European workers in the nineteenth and early twentieth centuries, to immigrants from Asia and Africa in the late twentieth century. Today, Warwick has a cosmopolitan population, made up of people from nearly every part of the world, each bringing its own heritage to mix with that already well established over the centuries.

The Theodore Francis Green Airport has grown to the extent that it has become one of the more significant facilities in Northeastern United States and is used by more than 5,000,000 passengers yearly. Along with the airport, Warwick abounds with a number of hotels, inns, and restaurants that thrive where once there were chickens, livestock, fruit trees, and unused land.

In 1932, the only thriving industry was the Apponaug Company; now there are many modern industries. Many businesses have found it prudent to take advantage of Warwick's location, and the Industrial Park along Jefferson Boulevard in Hillsgrove has given the city a much needed industrial base

Thanks in a great part with the coming of Routes I-95 and I-295 and the guidance of excellent political and business leaders, Warwick has become the "Retail Capital" of Rhode

Island. The city has two malls with over 100 stores and another 200 stores within a 3-mile stretch of Route 2.

The political scene is as exciting today as it was during the first mayoral race. When Warwick's mayor, Lincoln Chafee, became a U.S. senator upon the death of his father, John Chafee, a special election was called. Scott Avedisian, a Republican, was elected by a large majority.

Today, Warwick with a population exceeding 86,000 is Rhode Island's second largest city. It is conveniently located near all the major business, cultural, and recreation centers of New England. Providence is only ten minutes away; Boston, but one hour. Cape Cod can be reached in about 75 minutes, and the Connecticut casinos, in less than an hour. With the airport, interstate highways, and rail service, New York is easily reached, as are the ski slopes of the Northern states. Warwick is truly at "the Crossroads of New England."

Warwick's natural beauty along Greenwich Bay, its historical significance, and modern potential continue to attract tourists, businesses, movie producers, and those looking for the serenity of a suburban area with the advantages of a modern city. Warwick provides that and more.

Warwick's T.F. Green Airport is one of the fastest growing transportation centers in New England. Its state-of-the-art terminal and facilities have been highly praised by many passengers and airport officials.

1. THE BEGINNING

Warwick's written history begins with the purchase of the Shawomet lands by Samuel Gorton and 11 of his followers on January 12, 1642–43. The long prehistoric period, however, tells us that the area has been inhabited for much longer. Proof of this came in 1944 when a number of stone bowls, dishes, platters, pestles, mortars, and stone axes were found at the area called Pear Point in the Spring Green section of Warwick. These stone artifacts were made of steatite (soapstone) and were well over 2,000 years old. The discovery makes it clear that the use of stone bowls and pipes occurred long before John Greene Sr. purchased the lands from the Indian sachem, Socononoco, and before the written history of the area began.

By our modern time standards, these artifacts date to a dim and remote past, but in the geological time sense, they are recent indications of man's use of the land and materials in Warwick. Scientists and geologists inform us that, at one time, the 49.1 square miles we today call Warwick had a very different form and topography. Most of the city's 86,000 residents would find it difficult to imagine that at one time most of present-day Warwick, and much of Narragansett Bay, was covered by tundra, consisting of bushes with no trees, and a great deal of a variety of moss and lichen.

Both geological and political changes have left Warwick with a land area of 34.9 square miles, 14.2 square miles of inland waterways, and a 39-mile-long coastline. The city is essentially divided into two distinct areas consisting of a seaboard lowland section and an upland area, which contains Warwick's highest point: Spencer Hill, with an elevation of 350 feet above sea level. Situated at the center of the state's modern highway system and housing Rhode Island's largest airport, Warwick has witnessed tremendous industrial growth in recent decades with over 11 major industrial sites and more than 25 modern shopping centers.

The Wisconsin Glacier, dating back more than 20,000 years, had a dramatic effect upon the sea level. Archeologists believe that 8,600 years ago there was no bay, but just a river with rocky shores, and that earliest man paddled up this river in search of prehistoric game. Centuries later, these ancient hunters were followed by another wave of early man in search of the caribou that wandered over the area around 4,000 B.C. and in time, the tundra was replaced by forests and filled with deer, moose, fox, and other animals. During this period, the early ancestors of the Narragansett Indians arrived and, by 2,500 B.C., began to make tools and utensils from the stone quarries in nearby Oaklawn in Cranston.

The first European to glimpse the Warwick shore was Giovanni Da Verrazzano, who came to the area in 1524. The bas-relief stands near the Providence County Court House.

The first concrete evidence of Paleo-Indian man in New England comes from the finding of fluted points, which were used 10,000 years ago. During the long period between that date and the time of the first European contact, the environment of the early Indian changed from a cold, spruce-dominated landscape to a deciduous-forested environment. As a result, the methods of hunting and fishing changed, for along with the trees came animals such as the bear, deer, and the beaver, as well as an abundance of fish. This encouraged the establishment of semi-permanent villages in the area we today call Warwick.

By the time the first English settlers came to the area, the Narragansett Indians had established a definite pattern of civilization and fully utilized and managed the forests and the bay. In 1524, the Italian navigator Giovanni Verrazzano sailed into Narragansett Bay for the king of France. He was the first European to have set foot on the shores of Rhode Island. Fortunately, Verrazzano recorded where he had been and what he observed. The following is his description of the Narragansett Indians in the early sixteenth century: "This is the finest looking tribe, and the handsomest in their costumes, that we have found in our voyage . . . their faces are sharp, their hair long and black . . . their eyes are black and sharp, their expression mild and pleasant . . . We formed a great friendship with them."

As the American Indian in Warwick has no written language or recorded history, most of what we know about these early Americans has been passed to us from the writings of early explorers such as Verrazzano and the early English colonists. The studies of artifacts and village sites by modern archeologists and anthropologists have helped considerably in

13

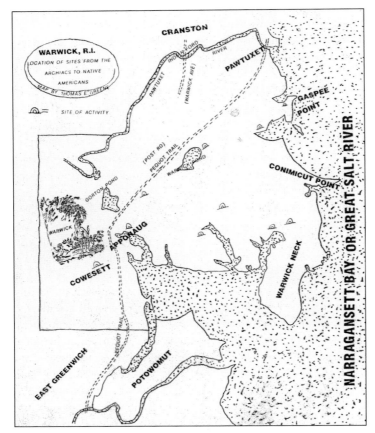

Archeologists report that the sites shown on this map were inhabited by American Indians prior to 1642. (Courtesy Thomas E. Greene.)

presenting a realistic portrayal of life in Warwick prior to 1642, but this material is limited and the history of the tribes is fragmentary. A great deal of our information of the tribes in Warwick comes from the writings of Roger Williams, Samuel Gorton, William Harris, and other colonists who carried with them many preconceived ideas of "the savages of the New World."

The colonist who stands out as the one who, according to his peers, had the greatest knowledge and understanding of the local Indians was Roger Williams, who took great pains in trying to understand the natives and was befriended by them. By his own admission, he owed his life to them on many occasions. His *Key Into the Language of America*, written in 1643, still remain the major source of information about the lifestyle of the native peoples before the impact of the colonists.

Samuel Gorton, Randall Holden, John Wickes, John Greene, and other Warwick settlers found many friends among the Narragansett Indians. In time, however, the excellent relations that existed between the colonists and the Indians began to deteriorate. Williams became disillusioned later in life and questioned whether it was possible for two such diverse cultures to coexist.

In Warwick, Samuel Gorton and his followers had problems in dealing with the Shawomets, a tribe living in the Warwick Neck area and part of the greater Narragansett unit. Much of the early writings of the Warwick colonists reflect complaints against Pomham, the Shawomet sachem. While the Indians inhabited the land for many millenniums before the coming of the Europeans, the two cultures only coexisted for little more than 34 years. In 1676, after King Philip's War, the might and power of the Narragansetts had been broken. Reverend Oliver Payson Fuller, in his *History of Warwick*, noted that from over 2,000 fighting men in 1676, the numbers were "reduced to 315" by 1766; and in 1832, while the number was the same, "only seven of them were of pure Indian blood." Fuller, citing Indian Commissioner E.R. Potter, recorded that there were no longer any full-blooded Narragansetts and concluded, "Thus in less than two centuries from the time that Roger Williams was greeted by the red man, with 'What Cheer, Netop' . . . the brave and hardy natives had nearly all passed away."

Even as early as the close of the eighteenth century, Warwick was totally an English colony, under control of English law and customs. The rich, colorful heritage of the American Indian has been nearly forgotten with little but place names such as Pawtuxet, Shawomet, Cowesett, and Potowomut to remind today's generations of the fascinating pre-colonial history of Warwick.

When the English immigrants began to settle in Warwick in 1642, differences between Europeans and American Indians were very obvious. The two cultures were separated by over 10,000 years of change. While man in America enjoyed the benefits of living in an environment with an abundance of game and maintained his existence by hunting and fishing, his European counterpart had, out of necessity, turned to agriculture. This activity in time led to the development of cities, written language, large armies, and increased trade.

The Indian had no such experience. His lifestyle had changed but little. He still found it possible to adapt to his environment, and his living continued to rely on hunting and fishing. Some differences from the earliest period in America were obvious, however, as the small family units became larger and bands and tribes were formed. Some agriculture and the pursuits of small animals in the woodland area, as well as the abundance of fish, made semi-permanent villages possible. Even before the Englishman settled in Warwick, the clash of cultures had begun. A plague in 1616–1617, most likely of European origin, severely crippled the Wampanoag Indians and altered the power balance and tribal hegemony in Rhode Island and Massachusetts.

By the time Roger Williams wrote his *Key Into the Language of America* in 1643, the Narragansett tribe had extended its power over most of Rhode Island. Their government, prior to the upheavals caused by the intrusion of the English and their culture, was well organized by class and title with clearly defined roles accepted by the members of the tribe. The Indians living in Warwick, known as the Shawomets, Pawtuxets, Cowesetts, and Potowomuts, were all subjects to the Narragansetts and, while they had their own sachems, or leaders, they recognized Canonicus and Miantonomi as their chief-sachems. The sachems performed the duties of chief judge and commander of the warriors. Williams noted that in addition to these chief-sachems were rulers called "Protectors, or under Sachims." In the Warwick area at the time of Williams and Gorton, Pomham and Socononaco were the under-sachems, or protectors, of the Shawomet and Pawtuxet tribes, and Taccomanan served the Potowomut tribe in that capacity.

The Indian was ruled by longstanding custom rather than by any written law. This proved to be a great disadvantage in dealing with the English, who had a very great respect for the written word and at times saw the lack of a written code among the Indians as an open invitation to reinterpretation and manipulation. In the case of the early land purchases, the so-called "Pawtuxet men" were able to challenge Gorton's purchase of the Shawomet territory by convincing under-sachems Pomham and Socononaco to make claims that Miantonomi had no legal right to sell the land.

All law, customs, religion, and rules were closely dependent upon the method by which the tribes derived their livelihood. According to Williams, the local Indians in Warwick basically would "hunt two wayes . . . [they] pursue their game . . . when they drive the woods before them." In the "masskill," the animals "were driven into a closed area by noise, fire, and shouting." The custom was to kill only enough to supply the tribe, and this slaughter was the main basis of their food supply. The local tribes also set traps, which they checked on a regular basis. Among the animals that were hunted in addition to the deer were beaver, foxes, otters, wild cats, and the dreaded wolf.

While hunting was the most important source of food supply, the Indian in Warwick also relied upon fishing, shellfishing, food gathering, and, to a limited extent, agriculture. The growing importance of farming as a means of supplementing the diet was apparent by the time of the first settlement of Warwick. Many of the fields were already cleared by both Indian men and women for planting. Once the ground was made ready, it became the responsibility of the women to plant, weed, and gather the corn, squashes, beans, and other crops. At times, as Williams writes, "the man himselfe, (either out of love to his

This summer wigwam is the type of dwelling in which the Native Americans in Warwick lived in during the seventeenth century.

A modern Wampanoag Indian is seen here recreating the environment of the time of contact with Europeans in early New England.

Wife, or care for his Children, or being an old man) will help the Woman which . . . they are not bound to." The one crop that the women were not allowed to plant and take care of was tobacco. The Indian male believed that the plant was a special gift given to them and that it had medicinal and perhaps magical qualities. The basic crop of corn was placed carefully in large baskets, dried, and later ground for use. The Indians also dried chestnuts and acorns, which they boiled, and used walnuts, strawberries, blueberries, and cranberries.

Because the Indian lived very close to nature, it was necessary for him to move as the seasons changed, and therefore he was discouraged from building a permanent or elaborate shelter. The Indians lived mostly in villages, which were constantly changing location.

While English writers noted that the houses were warm and that the Indians lived in some comfort, they fell far short of English standards. Roger Williams, who often stayed in these houses and whose life at times depended upon them, called them "filthy, smokey holes," and pointed out that in the summer they became infested with "the abundance of Fleas, which the dust of the house breeds." These simple, but efficient, houses served the Indian well and were left open most of the time, as the door usually consisted simply of a hanging mat. Their degree of hospitality and the idea that even strangers were welcome to enter their houses and share their food were a constant source of wonder to the English colonists.

The Indian mores and values differed from the colonists in many areas, but most obviously in the type of clothing. The Indian used clothes in a practical manner rather than for modesty or fashion. By English standards of the period, they were considered to be naked, and many Puritans felt that nakedness was in itself a sin.

The Narragansetts had developed a rather extensive and sophisticated trade long before the coming of the English colonists. While they did use the bartering system, they also had a form of currency usually called by the English, wampum. The Narragansetts were the principal makers of this type of currency in southern New England. This medium of exchange was made from quahaug shells, the value being not in the material used, but in the skill that went into making the beads, which were strung together.

Because of the lack of money in the early colonies, this wampum was used by the early settlers in Warwick as well as by the Indians. While the values varied, usually six of the small white beads in Williams's time were worth an English penny, and a fathom, made up of 360 beads, was worth 5 shillings. By 1663, the ease with which the Europeans could make wampum made it practically valueless, and in 1663 it ceased to be regarded by the colonists as legal tender.

The Indian had no wheel, no horse, or any beast of burden, and so they walked, ran, or went by canoe. In spite of these shortcomings, they were able to journey comparatively great distances. Travel by canoes, which were made of pine, oak, or chestnut, was often the preferred mode of movement. Even with stone tools, a skilled Indian could make a canoe within 12 days. They were expert in the maneuvering of these small craft and, because they were excellent swimmers, showed very little fear.

One of the great disadvantages that became obvious early in encounters with the English was the inferiority of their stone tools and weapons. Despite the handicap of the materials they worked with, the Indian showed a great ability to make the tools he needed, such as bows, arrows, and bowls, and had reached the stage of developing some pottery.

The area where English colonist and Native American seemed to be farthest apart was on the subject of organized religion. As most observations were made by Puritans during the early years of contact, the Indian religion was viewed as polytheistic and rife with devil-worship. As the Indian lived close to nature, he reasoned that nature and all natural phenomenon had a spiritual quality. Any excellence in man or animal was considered to be a sign of a "Manittoo," or a god. A great deal has been written on the Indian religion, with most writers concluding that Cowtantowit was regarded as their most powerful god, or good deity, and that he lived in the balmy regions of the Southwest. There was strong belief in the immortality of the soul and that there was a reward after death for those who led the proper life and punishment for those who did not.

The person who conducted religious ceremonies and guided the Indians was called a "shaman." Religion, hunting, morality, and many practical aspects of the Indian lifestyle were closely woven together, and the shaman was the expert in many of these areas. He interpreted the signs of nature, cured the sick and dying, and gave council to those in trouble. In their zeal to convert the Indian to Christianity, the English often sought to undermine the shaman. In doing so, they threatened the entire Indian culture, and this became a dominant problem in Indian-English relations.

A number of colonial writers, including Roger Williams, compared the Indians' morals very favorably to that of the English. "Drunkennesse and gluttony, generally they know not what sinnes they be" is an often quoted statement by Williams that presents the Indian as the victim of these European sins.

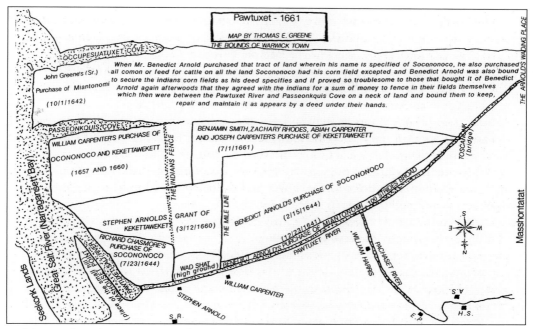

Maps such as these were were often drawn to ensure the legality of the purchases made by early colonists. (Courtesy Thomas E. Greene.)

Many English colonists found it difficult to understand the Indian concept of work and play. The Englishman regarded farming as a means of not only feeding his family, but of amassing wealth and gaining possessions. He believed, in many instances, that it was his "duty" to clear the land and farm it. The Indian, it appeared, left most of the planting and other aspects of agriculture to the female, as well as the tedious tasks of shellfishing. The Indian male, on the other hand, engaged primarily in hunting and fishing, areas the English regarded as supplemental or even recreational.

In the 40-year period of contact between Warwick's English colonists and the American Indian, the lifestyle of the latter was altered considerably. Within a short time, the communication between Indian and colonist greatly improved, as more of the colonists began to understand the language of the natives. In addition to Roger Williams, early Warwick settlers such as William and Benedict Arnold, John Greene Sr., and Samuel Gorton were known for their abilities as Indian interpreters.

The language, while not impossible to learn, was difficult, and many words had more than one meaning or had no equivalent in the English language. Difficulties in translation and frequent misunderstandings of land transfers caused many problems. As there was a great deal of land for their numbers and needs, large, cleared areas were left uncultivated for long periods of time. As a result, this fallow land was soon covered with berries and other wild plants, and became a feeding ground for deer and other wild animals. This was all part of the Indian pattern of farming, hunting, and gathering of food. The Englishmen misunderstood, and not realizing the Indian reliance on these areas, believed them to be vacant land and open for settlement.

Trade, for a number of years, proved beneficial to both English and Indian. Metal tools and utensils replaced stone and clay, and once dreary and difficult tasks became simple. Furs, as well as food, were eagerly exchanged for European goods. In time, however, the most sought after English goods, usually guns, gunpowder, and liquor, brought more detrimental than beneficial results.

Too late, the colonists in Warwick, realizing the devastating effects of the liquor on the Indians, tried to stop the trade. Despite laws such as those found in the Town Records, Book I, which stated, "no man in the towne is to sell strong lickers or sack to the Indians, for to drink in their houses, and if it bee proved, hee that so breaks this order shall pay to the treaserie five shillings for each offence," violations occurred frequently and coexistence became very difficult. O.P. Fuller tells us that complaints by the colonists were registered indicating, "the Indians had killed their cattle, entered their houses by force and committed other acts of violence."

Despite attempts by Samuel Gorton, John Greene, Roger Williams, Miantonomi, Canonicus, and other leaders of both colonists and Indians, relations deteriorated quickly. Repeated conflicts between Pomham and the Gortonists, as well as the horrors of King Philip's War, served to place the focus on the vices of both rather than the virtues. It soon became obvious that while both societies had their outstanding citizens who were known and respected for their virtues, they also had an assortment of liars, thieves, and murderers. Time proved that the Englishman was not a God bringing great benefits of civilization to his American contemporary and neither was the Indian a "noble savage," living in a simple, tranquil world. The Indian was a human being who loved, hated, laughed, and cried. His lifestyle was relatively simple in comparison to that of the European, and while the technological differences placed him far apart, his human qualities, positive and negative, were not so different.

At the Lambert Farm in Cowesett (1988–1990), members of the Public Archeology Laboratory, Inc. uncovered artifacts indicating the presence of the American Indian in the area prior to 1642. (Courtesy Gary Melino.)

2. WARWICK'S COLONIAL HISTORY

Warwick's colonial history, which covers the period between 1642 and 1776, is as fascinating as it is long. From the very beginning, turmoil and controversy were constant factors in the development of the colony. While Warwick is usually regarded as the Gorton colony, Samuel Gorton was not the first to settle there. Prior to his arrival, William Arnold, William Harris, Robert Cole, and John Greene Sr. had already settled along the banks of the Pawtuxet River. John Greene very early befriended Gorton and his followers, but Arnold and Harris were determined to stop the Gortonists from settling in the area.

In comparing Samuel Gorton to Roger Williams, Reverend O.P. Fuller commented that "Gorton was also a preacher and founder of a religious sect, and his views, both ecclesiastical and political, were not only obnoxious to the colonists of Massachusetts but also in a lesser degree to those of Providence and Aquidneck." Fuller believed that both Williams and Gorton "had sought the more hospitable regions among the Indians where they hoped quietly to enjoy that freedom in 'religious concernments' which they were denied among their own countrymen."

Samuel Gorton arrived at Boston from London in 1636. Realizing that Puritanical Boston was attempting to control all religious thought, Gorton moved to Plymouth, where he hoped he would be allowed greater freedom. In Plymouth, he met with some success and began to attract a number of followers. It was soon obvious that Gorton's religious concepts differed a great deal from those of Ralph Smith, a former minister in Plymouth, from whom Gorton had rented a house. When a number of members of Smith's household began attending services conducted by Gorton, Smith attempted to have Gorton evicted. Very quickly, an additional problem arose when one of Gorton's female servants was seen "to smile in church." This was considered a very serious offense in the Plymouth colony, and Samuel Gorton went to her defense. While defending his servant in court, Gorton was charged with "conducting himself in a very rude and contemptuous manner." This eventually led to Gorton's leaving Plymouth for Aquidneck Island.

Gorton's strong stand against attempts by the Plymouth court to suppress his religious convictions at first made him very welcome on Aquidneck Island in 1638. At this time, he was accompanied by John Wickes, one of his earlier followers, and in a short time attracted the loyalty of "Richard Carder, Randall Holden, Sampson Shatton and Robert

Potter" to his cause. Within a very short time, Gorton and his followers were considered undesirable on Aquidneck Island, as they refused to adhere to that colony's laws. In Portsmouth, the catalyst was an old woman whose cow had trespassed on Gorton's land. She alleged that one of Gorton's maidservants had assaulted her so she complained to Nicholas Easton, the deputy governor. Gorton attempted to defend his maidservant in the Aquidneck court and, according to the charges against him, Gorton became very abusive when Governor William Coddington attempted to sum up the case before the jury. There were 14 charges, and they included the following:

> That Samuel Gorton contumeliously reproached the Magistrates, calling them Just Asses . . . The said Gorton charged the Deputy Governor to be an Abetter of a Riot, Assault, or Battery and professed that he would not touch him, no, not with a pair of tongs . . .

As a result of this action, Gorton was sentenced to be whipped and was banished from the island in March or April 1640. From Aquidneck Island, Gorton and his followers proceeded to Providence. Once in Providence, Gorton attracted many of the dissidents there, became their leader and spokesman, and once again became the center of controversy.

Roger Williams, in a letter to Governor Winthrop, dated Providence 1640, wrote, "Master Gorton having abused high and low at Aquidnick, is now bewitching and bemadding poor Providence, with his uncleane and foul censures of all the ministers of this country, . . . and also denying all visible and externall ordinances." Williams and a few others refused to admit Gorton as an inhabitant with town privileges. Despite this opposition, Gorton's followers grew, causing Williams to remark to Winthrop, "Yet the tide is too strong against us, and I feare it will force me to little Patience, a little isle next to your Prudence."

The differences between Williams and Gorton were not on religious grounds but on the question of the concept of government. Gorton, in 1641, again attempted to be received in "town fellowship" and again he was refused. The man who most strenuously opposed Gorton's application at this time was William Arnold, who asserted that Gorton was "an insolent, railing and turbulent person" and that he had divided Providence "into parties aiming to drive away its founders."

The bitter feelings that grew between Arnold and Gorton lasted for the lifetime of both men and were responsible for many of the disturbing events of the early period. Serious difficulties arose in Providence in November 1641, when a group of "eight men orderly chosen" rendered a decision against one of Gorton's followers, Francis Weston, and attempted to confiscate his cattle. The Gortonists, which included Samuel Gorton, John Greene, and Randall Holden, rallied behind Weston and rescued him and his cattle. A riot occurred as a result and blood was shed. Arnold and 12 others protested, and when Gorton and his followers moved into the Pawtuxet area, three of the original Pawtuxet purchasers, William Arnold, Robert Cole, William Carpenter, as well as Benedict Arnold, William Arnold's son, offered themselves and their land to the protection of Massachusetts in September 1642. The Gortonists became alarmed over the possibility of

Unfortunately, no portrait or statue of Samuel Gorton exists. In 1939, the City of Warwick dedicated one of its high schools in his honor. Today, the Samuel Gorton High School, now a junior high, is an excellent visual reminder of Warwick's founder.

intervention by Massachusetts. They wrote a letter "To our neighbors of Massachusetts," which, according to nineteenth-century historian Samuel Greene Arnold, "heaped a storm of theological invective" on the authorities there.

The Gortonists then moved to the land south of Pawtuxet called Shawomet to be beyond the limits of Providence and Pawtuxet. Here, in November 1642, they purchased the lands now known as Warwick, West Warwick, and Coventry from the Indians. Gorton's bitter letter of rebuke to Massachusetts made him several powerful enemies among the Massachusetts magistrates and became the basis for later charges of heresy.

On January 12, 1642–43, Gorton and 11 of his followers signed a deed known as the Shawomet Purchase with Miantonomi, the "chief Sachem of the Narragansetts." This deed was witnessed by Pomham, the sachem of Shawomet, and a number of others. The purchase included about 90 square miles of territory, or approximately 60,000 acres. All of the present city of Warwick, with the exception of Potowomut and the northeast corner along the Pawtuxet River, was included.

The northeast area of present-day Warwick, called Occupastuxet, later Spring Green, and Governor Francis Farms, was purchased earlier by Surgeon John Greene from Miantonomi and Socononoco, the sachem of Pawtuxet. This purchase, according to Warwick Town Records, was dated October 4, 1642, and was confirmed by Susquans, alias Moosup, to Deputy Governor John Greene, June 6, 1662.

The price paid for the Shawomet lands, according to the deed, was "one hundred and forty foure fathoms of wampumpeage." The original deed lists the purchasers as "Randall Houlden, John Greene, John Wickes, Francis Weston, Samuel Gorton, Richard Waterman, John Warner, Richard Carder, Sampson Shotten, William Wuddall." According to historian S.G. Arnold, Nicholas Powers, not mentioned in the deed, was also one of the purchasers.

The attack by Massachusetts soldiers on the Gortonists in Shawomet in 1643 has been called one of the greatest crimes of the colonial period.

The "Pawtuxet Men," led by William Arnold, quickly hoped to drive Gorton from Shawomet. Along with the Massachusetts authorities, they convinced Pomham, the sachem of Shawomet, and Socon)noco, the sachem of Pawtuxet, to place their lands under the Massachusetts jurisdiction and to deny that they had assented to Miantonomi's sale of the lands to the Gortonists. Historian Samuel G. Arnold, in evaluating these proceedings, wrote, "this act of submission afforded another pretext, . . . to harass the unhappy Gortonists in this their last retreat," as Massachusetts claimed an act of submission to their government by any party extended their jurisdiction over that party's lands.

Acting on the submission of Pomham and Socononoco, the Massachusetts General Court sent a letter to the purchasers of Shawomet demanding their presence before the court. In September 1643, a letter signed by Randall Holden, but most likely written by Samuel Gorton, answered the Massachusetts demand. It denounced Pomham's conduct, charging that the Indians under the "shield of Massachusetts" were committing outrages against them. This letter, as might be expected, infuriated the Massachusetts General Court, which had already been subjected to Gorton's scorn and ridicule. According to S.G. Arnold, they took action by sending "Capt. Cook, Lieut. Atherton, and Edward Johnson with forty soldiers to Warwick." Arnold goes on to say that, fearing the worst, the Shawomet settlers sent their women and children "some to the woods and others in boats to gain the [safety of] the neighboring plantations." As soon as they felt their families were safe, the men fortified one of the houses and prepared to defend it. The troops from Massachusetts arrived, accompanied by four Providence men, who tried to negotiate a peaceful settlement. This move was to no avail.

On October 3, 1643, the cattle of the Shawomet men were seized and the assault began. After several days, as the troops were pressing closer and closer to the house, the Gortonists felt they had no choice but to surrender to the superior force. The action that followed has been described as one of the most disgraceful episodes in English colonial history. Gorton and his followers were roughly handled and carried off as prisoners to Boston.

The Gortonists were tried on charges of "heresy and sedition." Samuel Gorton was found guilty and all but three of the magistrates called for the death sentence. Fortunately, the majority of deputies refused to sanction the penalty. Gorton and six of his followers (Wickes, Holden, Potter, Carder, Weston, and Warner) were put in irons and set to work in various towns. Waterman, Waddell, and Power were given milder treatment and allowed to go free in a short time. After a very humiliating and brutal winter, Gorton and his men were set free, but banished from all territory under the jurisdiction of Massachusetts and Plymouth Colonies. They claimed this included Providence and the "lands of the subject Indians." Gorton asked if this included Shawomet, and he was told it did and that Gorton had to leave there or he would be put to death.

The Gortonists again found refuge on Aquidneck Island. Here, despite the fact that he had been banished earlier, Gorton was welcomed for his cause and the obvious mistreatment he received from the Massachusetts Bay Colony. The results of the unjust seizure and sentencing of the Gortonists not only changed the attitude of the colonists on Aquidneck Island, but it also had an effect upon the Indians. They were amazed that Gorton was set free and believed that the "Gortonoges," as they called them, had more powerful friends in England than did the English of Massachusetts, whom they called "Wattaconoges," the people who wore coats.

Through treachery and with the aid and assistance of Massachusetts, the Narragansett Sachem Miantonomi had been brutally murdered by Uncas, the Mohegan, while Gorton was held prisoner. Believing that Gorton was a friend of Miantonomi and had great influence in the English Court, the tribe placed itself under "the government and protection of that honorable State of Old England," and made Gorton, Wicks, Holden, and Warner their agents to report their submission to the king. During the winter of 1644–45, Gorton, accompanied by Randall Holden and John Greene, set sail for England.

Before any Massachusetts or Plymouth colonists made claims to the land, Samuel Gorton was able to present his case before Parliament. There, thanks to the influence of Robert Rich, Earl of Warwick and Governor-in-Chief of Foreign Plantations, the lands were restored to Gorton and his followers. Randall Holden returned to Boston on September 13, 1646, with an order requiring Massachusetts to reinstate the Shawomet purchasers and forbidding any attempt by Massachusetts to exercise jurisdiction over them. In honor of the earl, and in gratitude, Gorton changed the name of the colony from "Shawomet" to "Warwick."

SIMPLICITIES DEFENCE
against
SEVEN-HEADED POLICY.
OR
A true complaint of a peaceable people, being part of the English in New England, made unto the state of Old England, against cruell persecutors

United in Church-Government
in those parts.

Wherein is made manifest the manifold out-rages cruelties, oppressions, and taxations, by cruell and close imprisonments, fire and sword, deprivation of goods, Lands, and livelyhood, and such like barbarous inhumanities, exercised upon the people of Providence plantations in the Nanhyganset Bay by those of the Massachusets, with the rest of the united Colonies, stretching themselves beyond the bounds of all their own jurisdictions, perpetrated and acted in such an unreasonable and barbarous manner, as many thereby have lost their lives.

As it hath been faithfully declared to the Honourable Committee of Lords and Commons for Forrain Plantations, whereupon they gave present Order for Redress.

The sight and consideration whereof hath moved a great Country of the Indians and Natives in those parts, Princes and people to submit unto the Crown of England, and earnestly to sue to the State thereof for safeguard and shelter from like cruelties.

Imprimatur, Aug. 3d. 1646. Diligently perused, approved, and Licensed to the Presse, according to Order by publike Authority.

LONDON,
Printed by John Macock, and are to be sold by George Whittington at the blue Anchor neer the Royal Exchange in Cornhil. 1647.

Samuel Gorton's Simplicities Defence *poured scorn and ridicule upon his enemies. This pamphlet was printed in London in 1647.*

Once again settled in their lands, the Gortonists struggled over the problem of establishing a legal government. A charter for Rhode Island and Providence Plantations was adopted on March 19, 1647, and Warwick was shortly thereafter included. Once this transpired, the colonists in Warwick cooperated fully. Randall Holden was named "Assistant from Warwick" (an office corresponding to that of state senator today), and six men were selected to represent the town in the General Assembly. Warwick's Town Charter was adopted on March 14, 1648, and a town council, consisting of John Greene, Ezekiel Holliman, John Warner, Rufus Barton, John Wickes, and Randall Holden, was established. Rufus Barton and John Wickes were named magistrates, John Warner became the first town clerk, Henry Townsend was named constable, and Christopher Heime, one of the "received inhabitants," was appointed as town sergeant.

Warwick's first book of records, covering the years 1647 to 1667, provides an excellent description of some of the laws, customs, problems, and mores of the very early period of settlement. From it can be seen that town council meetings were held "ye first Monday in every moonth," and that "if 12 Townsmen met in one day appointed for Towne meeting, they shall have power to act in Towne affairs as though all were present." We also learn that, during this early period, many regarded public office as a burden rather than an honor. Because so many were reluctant to give time and effort to the management of the town, penalties had to be levied against those who refused to serve.

There were many dangers in the early period. One of which was the fear of attacks by various enemies. As a result, a number of military measures were passed. To provide for the common defense, men were organized in "Training Bands," a type of early militia, which were to meet on the first Tuesday after the 12th day of March. While the band was made up of men from 17 to 70, military training began at a very young age. It was the responsibility of every father in the colony to begin training his sons at age seven.

The Warwick men attributed the most vexing problems of the period from 1648 to 1675 to the Pawtuxet and Shawomet Indians. In 1648, John Smith, on behalf of Warwick, complained to the New England Commissioners that "the Indians had killed their cattle, entered their houses by force and had committed other acts of violence." The arch-villain from the Warwick colonists' point-of-view was Pomham, the Shawomet sachem who refused to leave his lands on Warwick Neck. After Miantonomi had been killed, Pomham, fearing the Narragansetts would accuse him of treason and that he would be attacked, asked the Massachusetts Bay Colony for assistance. According to O.P. Fuller, "an officer and ten soldiers had been sent to assist Pomham to build a fort and remain with them until the danger was over." "Tradition," he says, "locates this fort on the east bank of Warwick Cove, nearly opposite the Oakland Beach grounds in the estate of John Holden."

By 1665, the King's Commissioners ordered that "Pumham and the Indians with him shall plant their corne this year . . . and that before the next planting time, he, and all the

The oldest meeting house in Warwick was this Six-Principle Baptist Church, which dated back to the early eighteenth century. It was torn down in 1830.

Indians with him shall remove to some other place." An agreement was made with the Indians on Warwick Neck and signed by Cheesechamut, son of Pomham, to leave upon payment of a sum of money by the colonists. Pomham received the agreed-upon sum, but remained in the area in violation of the agreement. It was not until King Philip's War in 1675–76, that Pomham eventually left Warwick Neck.

Not all problems were confined to Pomham and the Indians, however. During the early period, there was a great danger and nuisance from wolves, bears, gray squirrels, rats, and wild cats. Bounties, ranging from 1 shilling to 5 pounds, were paid in an effort to rid the area of the pests. One entry in the Town Records dated October 10, 1658, states, "that if anyone kill the great gray woolfe that hath done so much mischiefe in the Towne hee shall have five pounds for his pains and for an other woolfe fower pounds."

One of the more serious problems dealt with the sale of liquor to the Indians. One law stated that "no man in the towne is to sell strong lickers or sack to the Indians." Unfortunately, this didn't stop the illegal sales even when the fine was increased to 20 shillings, and beer and wine were added to the list of goods prohibited for sale to the Indians.

On February 3, 1651, there was an "Agreement between the Towne of Waraicke with Mr. John Wickes, Mr. Randall Houlden, Mr. Walter Todd, John Greene, Jr., as undertakers to build a mill in the aforesaide Towne." They were given permission to "damme up the fresh river for their use." The mill owners had agreed to grind their own

This is a sketch by Mrs. John Wickes Greene of Randall Holden's residence. In 1644, Randall Holden, accompanied by John Greene Sr. and Samuel Gorton, went to England and successfully persuaded the Earl of Warwick to champion their cause against Massachusetts Bay Colony.

corn at the rate of 2 quarts per bushel, which seemed fair. Within a short time, however, the Records tell us that "It being complained of that the Toll Dish is too bigg" and the Town ordered that a "pair of skaills [scales] for the mill" be obtained.

Land, while plentiful and cheap, became one of the chief areas of dissension. Along with the original purchasers, individuals were allowed to become "inhabitants," and could purchase land. An "inhabitant," who paid a sum of 10 pounds and was received into the town by a formal vote, was entitled to all the rights and privileges of the original purchasers. O.P Fuller tells us that "By far the larger number of acts passed by the town up to this time related to the disposition of the lands." The grants were generally of 6 acres as house lots and greater amounts could be purchased.

From the time Samuel Gorton returned to America in 1648 until his death in 1677, his small colony grew slowly and sometimes painfully, often embroiled in the life and death struggles of politics, economics, Indian warfare, and land divisions. While Samuel Gorton was still in England countering claims by Massachusetts against the colony, Warwick was chartered in 1648 as one of the "four towns" of the "Providence Plantations in Narragansett." Under the 1644 charter, a General Assembly, at first made up of all freemen and later of 40 representatives, was established. A ruling body of ten men, as a general court headed by a president and four assistants, was chosen. John Coggeshall, of Newport, was the first president, and Randall Holden was selected as assistant from Warwick. The Pawtuxet men were asked to join, but they refused, claiming to be under the jurisdiction of Massachusetts.

Upon his return to Shawomet, which he now called Warwick, Gorton found his followers settled around the head of Warwick Cove, and the hostile Pomham and his Indians firmly entrenched at Warwick Neck. Each settler was given a small portion of territory as a house lot with the provision that a dwelling should be erected on the site within six months of the grant.

By 1650, lots of land, usually of 6 acres, were allocated to the original purchasers and to 31 "inhabitants." Divisions of the "Four Mile Common," which extended from the "head of the Neck" to Apponaug, began at this time with lots assigned in the Conimicut section. This division was not completed until 1748. The original purchasers retained claim to Warwick Neck for themselves, and Occupassnestuxet, while politically part of the town, was in the private possession of John Greene.

Difficulties concerning the Pawtuxet lands and dealings with Massachusetts, which claimed the Warwick lands should be under the control of Plymouth, continued. This caused the General Assembly to ask Roger Williams to return to England to safeguard the colony's interests. Warwick, being especially affected, raised money totaling 100 pounds to help pay the expenses of the trip. Even with this and other donations, Roger Williams was forced to sell his "trading house" in Narragansett to sustain his wife and family while he was gone. In 1651, because of the claims of William Coddington, the founder of Newport, Aquidneck Island withdrew from the towns of Providence and Warwick. The reduced General Assembly met in Warwick as usual that year and elected Samuel Gorton as president and John Greene as clerk of the Assembly. In an attempt to prevent further encroachment on Rhode Island, a law was passed during this session forbidding the purchase of land from the Indians without consent of the Assembly.

Canonchet, the last sachem of the Narragansett Indians, gave aid to the Wampanoags in King Philip's War. This leader brought the wrath of the English colonists in Massachusetts upon his tribe in Rhode Island.

During the following session, in which Samuel Gorton was a general assistant from Warwick and moderator of the General Court and John Greene was secretary, a law was passed against slavery. It stated as follows:

> let it be ordered, that no blacke mankind or white being forced by covenant bond, or otherwise, to serve any man . . . longer than ten yeares. . . . At the end or terme of ten yeares to self them free, as the manner is with the English servants.

Warwick during this time had been engaged in an active trade with the Dutch at Manhattan. It was common for the crew of the Dutch vessels to stay in Warwick until their goods were sold and they were able to purchase a cargo for the return to Manhattan. In 1652, one of these crews took room and board with John Warner, Warwick's first town clerk and a magistrate of the town. When it came time to settle accounts, Warner and the Dutch disagreed. In the violent debate that followed, Warner was brought before the court. He refused to cooperate and at a town meeting he was disenfranchised. According to the first book of Town Records, Warner made a series of accusations against the town and called the town officers "rogues and thieves" and threatened to "beate out their braines."

In July 1654, there was cause for optimism as the Town purchased Potowomut from the Sachem Taccomanan "for ye just some of fifteen pounds dewly paid and received already, in wampumpeage; only I am to receive ye value of one coate of such cloth as ye Indians doe now commonly use to weare, annually as a gratuity hereafter."

While the town of Warwick was able to make progress politically and economically, the problems between the Gortonists and the Shawomet Indians were not resolved until after King Philip's War. Despite the hostile feelings of the settlers regarding Pomham, the Gortonists hoped to avoid an open conflict. When the Wampanoag sachem Metacomet (King Philip) and the Massachusetts Bay Colony went to war in June 1675, most Rhode Island settlers and the Narragansett Indians hoped to remain neutral. Non-involvement proved to be impossible, however, once the fighting began.

The Indian warriors under Philip were very successful during the early months of the war but, as the winter approached, they began to lose momentum, and Philip soon needed a safe haven for his women, children, sick, and wounded. He asked Canonchet, chief sachem of the Narragansetts, for assistance. The Narragansetts were very powerful and had a fort in the Great Swamp in South Kingstown, which they believed was impenetrable.

Despite threats by the Massachusetts commissioners, Canonchet agreed to harbor the Wampanoags and, as a result, the war was brought to Rhode Island. Armies from Massachusetts Bay, Plymouth, and Connecticut invaded the small colony in December 1675. Word was sent to Warwick at this time, advising the citizens there of the plans and cautioning them to be on guard against possible retaliation. Plans were made in Warwick to move the women, children, old, and infirm to the islands as quickly as possible. While most agreed, some refused to leave the land they considered home.

One who was very reluctant to seek safety was the controversial founder of Pawtuxet, 90-year-old William Arnold. Samuel Gorton, age 83 at the time, was also reluctant to leave. Eventually, friendly Indians were able to persuade Gorton to allow them to take him to the safety of Prudence Island.

Early in December 1675, over 1,000 men from Massachusetts Bay, Plymouth, and Connecticut arrived at Smith's Garrison at Cocumscussoc, a little north of Wickford. These troops, under the command of General Josiah Winslow, governor of Plymouth, were the largest force New England had ever seen.

The majority of troops crossed the Seekonk River and followed the old Pequot Path to Pawtuxet. While here, Winslow received word that Pomham was still in Warwick. In hopes of trapping the Shawomet sachem, Winslow ordered a night march into Warwick on December 12. Winslow's guides, hampered by bitter cold and darkness, lost their way. By daybreak, the troops were still short of their mark, and the clever Pomham had easily escaped the trap. The English troops eventually reached Smith's Castle and on December 18, 1675, proceeded through heavy snow and bitter cold to attack Canonchet's fort in the Great Swamp.

The action that took place in the Great Swamp in South Kingstown was the most significant battle of the King Philip's War and also the most horrible. The colonists were successful in penetrating the defenses of the Narragansetts and once inside the walls set fire to the 500 wigwams in the fort. Many women and children died as a result. When it was over, the Narragansett Indian tribe was devastated and was never again a powerful force in New England.

The Indian warriors who managed to escape the slaughter wreaked havoc on Rhode Island, burning and killing in retaliation. The only success the colonists had during late December was in a raid on Pomham's village near Warwick and the capture of a renegade white man, Joshua Tefft, near Providence. Samuel Greene Arnold, in his *History of Rhode Island*, noted the following:

> Warwick . . . left defenceless by the retiring army, was abandoned, and the inhabitants took refuge on the island, where their town meetings were regularly held, as if at home for the choice of deputies and jurors. The town was annihilated for the time, but the corporation survived, and continued to discharge its legitimate functions. . . .
>
> The Indians fled at the approach of the English, and retreated northward, driving off the livestock from Warwick. The army pursued them but a few miles, and soon after returned home and was disbanded.

From late January until April 1676, most of the victories were on the side of the Indians. On January 27, 1676, the Indians attacked Pawtuxet. William Harris witnessed this raid and in his letter on the war relates that during this attack, he lost his youngest son, 30-year-old Toleration Harris. Approximately 300 Indians attacked William Carpenter's farm in Pawtuxet, burning outbuildings, corn, and hay, and driving away 180 sheep, 50 head of cattle, and large number of horses. William Harris wrote the following of the attack:

> I have lost a dear son. He was a diligent talented, just man, temperate in all things, whom the Indians lay in wait for by the road and killed, along with a Negro man. They also burned our houses, drove away about fifty head of cowkind cattle and eighty horses . . . and burned more than fifty loads of hay.

Thomas Greene's Stone Castle, built by John Smith in 1649, was the only building in Warwick not burned to the ground in King Philip's War. The house was demolished in 1795.

William Hubbard, a Massachusetts clergyman writing in 1677, recorded that Warwick was "all of it burned by the enemy at several times"; Pawtuxet had "twelve houses burned in the beginning of March, 1676"; and Providence had "eighteen houses burned, June 28, 1675." Despite the setbacks during the early months of 1676, the colonists were witnessing the gradual destruction of the Indian. Each day meant greater sufferings and starvation for the Narragansetts, as they were unable to maintain their villages.

In June, any hope the Narragansetts may have had of negotiating for peace ended. The Narragansett Sachem Potuck, with about 80 warriors, reached Providence in June. He indicated his willingness to stop fighting and was persuaded by Roger Williams, Arthur Fenner, and John Greene of Warwick to go to Newport to negotiate. He was promised by these men that in three days time he would be able to return to join his men at Warwick Neck. Potuck agreed and was taken to Aquidneck Island in John Greene's sloop.

In Newport, instead of being treated with respect, Potuck was seized and made prisoner, eventually sent to Boston and executed. Captain John Talcott, with 300 English soldiers and Indian allies, marched to Warwick from Connecticut in July 1676. Talcott's men attacked a large body of Narragansetts camped along the south branch of the Pawtuxet River, probably near Natick. Over 170 Indians, including women and children, were killed or taken prisoner. Following this victory, Talcott received word that 80 of Potuck's warriors were on Warwick Neck. Completely disregarding the promises of safety made to Potuck by Williams and Greene, Talcott attacked the Narragansetts at Warwick Neck on July 3, 1676, killing, wounding, or capturing 67 of them.

The last significant fighting in the Rhode Island area occurred on July 25, when the chief antagonist of the Gortonists in Warwick, the Shawomet Sachem Pomham was killed. The wily old sachem had led his starving band of warriors on an attack at Medfield, Massachusetts. He was chased by the English to Mendon, about 20 miles north of Providence. The Indians were decisively defeated in the battle that followed, and Pomham was knocked to the ground by a bullet. Somehow, he managed to crawl off to one side and when one of the soldiers, believing the old man was nearly dead came too close, Pomham seized the young soldier in a death grip and nearly killed him before comrades came to his rescue.

By October 1676, all the major Indian leaders had been killed or captured and the war was over. Slowly, Warwick's residents began to return to rebuild and to start a new phase in the colony's development.

In his 1875 history of Warwick, O.P. Fuller noted the following:

> The war being now over the people of Warwick in the spring of 1677 returned to their desolated homes, and with hearts undaunted commenced at once to repair their wasted heritage. . . . The Indians were now timid and suppliant, rather than bold and threatening . . .

Once the threat of Indian uprisings was removed, it was possible to settle the lands west of Apponaug and to move into the previously unsettled lands of the Grand or Shawomet Purchase.

The James Greene house in Buttonwoods, with its large brick chimney, still stands in Warwick. The original section was built in the late seventeenth century and is one of Warwick's oldest homes. It has been restored and renovated by Steve and Jean Tyson.

With an increase in population and an end of Indian problems, it became obvious that if the town was to grow and supply the needs of its people, the waterpower and other resources to the west would have to be developed. The old sawmill at Tuskatucket Brook (at the head of Brush Neck Cove) was not adequate to meet the demands of the inhabitants, and early in 1677–78, a grant was made to establish a sawmill along the Pawtuxet River.

By 1696, it was deemed necessary to establish a fulling mill, which would shrink and thicken woolen cloth to make it more satisfactory for use in clothing. Fuller's earth or clay, which was a catalyst in this process, was found at Apponaug, and a fuller, John Micarter, was given an acre and a half of land in that village and permission to build a mill to "do the town's work upon as reasonable terms as they can have it done elsewhere."

Between 1677 and 1750, the land of the Shawomet and Potowomut Purchases was divided and allocated among the proprietors of Warwick. In 1680, the number was fixed at 51 and consisted of "original purchasers," "purchasers" who gave 10 pounds into the common treasury, and "inhabitants." These applicants, designated as "inhabitants," upon receiving a favorable vote of admission by "papers or beans," and upon the payment of 12 shillings to the treasury, "received a home lot of six acres and the right to share equally with all the other proprietors in the land set aside as the Four Mile Common."

Between 1656 and 1680, most of the shares of land at Potowomut were acquired by the Greene family. The Greenes originally had four shares, but by marriage and other arrangements came to own nearly all of the area. Previous to 1684, the land was not occupied and was used primarily to raise cattle. Much of the hay gathered from the meadows and grassy fields was taken across Greenwich Bay to a town wharf, which was built on Richard Carder's land (present-day Wharf Road in Old Warwick Cove) for that purpose.

In 1684, James Greene (1626–1698), one of the sons of Surgeon John Greene, and his nephew, Thomas Greene, settled in the area. James Greene built his home on the crest of a hill looking east to the river at its base, and Thomas Greene built his residence at the mouth of the Potowomut River. The development of these two sites by the Greene family has had a very significant effect on Warwick's history. James' son, Jabez (1673–1741), and Thomas Hill, who owned the property across the river, built a dam, which provided the power to run a saw and gristmill.

Jabez, an early Quaker, was very successful, and his holdings included, in addition to a dam, forge, and sawmill, a number of dwellings, barns, warehouses, a store, and an anchor works. His son, Nathanael Greene Sr. (1707–1768), eventually controlled most of the property by purchasing his brothers' share of the forge and mills, and in 1763, he was the second highest taxpayer in Warwick. The Greene brothers started an additional enterprise in 1741 along the southern branch of the Pawtuxet River in what is today the Quidnick-Anthony section of Coventry. Nathanael Greene Jr., Rhode Island's most illustrious Revolutionary War hero, was placed in charge of this thriving enterprise in 1768.

While some areas such as Potowomut were settled with little difficulty, other sections required many years and extensive litigation before the boundaries were settled. Throughout much of the late seventeenth and early eighteenth centuries, constant problems arose between the Gortonists and William Harris over the ownership of Pawtuxet lands and meadows. Harris, one of the colony's most able but controversial figures, won a number of judgments against Warwick, but was unable to enforce his claims. As long as William Harris was alive, however, very little progress was made in settling of the ownership of the Pawtuxet lands, and his death marked the beginning of the end of the long struggle.

The Nathanael Greene birthplace in Potowomut dates to 1684. The elderly gentleman sitting in front of the house is Judge Richard Ward Greene, who died in 1875.

In 1696, the Pawtuxet River was determined as the boundary between Warwick and Providence and, by 1714, after both Roger Williams and William Harris were dead, the final boundaries of the Pawtuxet Purchase were settled. In 1754, Cranston was separated from Providence, and Pawtuxet north of the river became part of the newly created town.

In 1708, the census reports listed the population of Rhode Island as 7,181 and of Warwick as 480. By this date, all of the original settlers of the four towns had died. Among the last were Roger Williams (1683) and Randall Holden (1692). Warwick's early families continued to take an active part in the colony's politics. John Greene Jr., who had served as general recorder for Providence and Warwick from 1652 to 1654 and 1657 to 1660, was elected as "Major for the mainland" from 1684 to 1689, and was deputy governor from May 1690 to May 1700. During the early eighteenth century, a number of Warwick men served as Speakers of the House of Representatives in the General Assembly. They were Benjamin Barton (1703–1704), James Greene (1707, 1711–12), Simon Smith (1709), and Randall Holden (1714–1715).

Major political changes occurred in the colony when King Charles II died and James II replaced him. King James, who exhibited little understanding of the needs and wants of the colonies, appointed Sir Edmund Andros as royal governor for all the New England colonies. As a result, Rhode Island lost many of the rights and privileges that had been granted her by the Charter of 1663. All of Rhode Island was declared to be one county, and Major John Greene Jr. of Warwick, one of the first to be elected to the position of major, was commissioned to carry letters to England and to act as the colony's agent.

The "Glorious," or "Bloodless," Revolution of 1688 brought Andros's control to an end as William and Mary became rulers of England, replacing the unpopular James II. The era that began with William and Mary marked the time that Warwick, like all of Rhode Island, came into its own in agriculture and trade. Warwick was able to overcome its internal problems, settling its western border with Connecticut and satisfactorily ending the Pawtuxet claims.

By the end of the period, the towns in the Rhode Island colony numbered 21, and Warwick, the town that had caused so much friction in the time of Samuel Gorton, was able to live in harmony with her neighbors. Part of the reason for the harmony was that the reign of William and Mary brought about the Toleration Act for Religion and an English Bill of Rights for politics. This greatly reduced the religious animosity that once made the Gortonists objects of the wrath of other colonies and helped promote the concepts of political freedom that Warwick advocated from its early days. During this period, Warwick increased her agricultural products by the settling of the Cowesett division, the Wecochaconet Farms, and the Natick Lands.

The colony also became a significant part of the ever-growing sea trade. Much of this was due to the leadership of Major John Greene Jr. He was annually elected deputy governor from 1690 to 1700 and served during the terms of Governors John Easton, Caleb Carr, Walter Dark, and Samuel Cranston. As deputy governor, Major Greene received no salary but he was exempted from paying taxes.

During his tenure in that office, the town of Warwick was nearly destroyed by a smallpox epidemic in 1690–91, witnessed the introduction of paper money as bills of credit, and welcomed the beginnings of a post office. Greene journeyed to Boston in

This lovely home, demolished in 1946 as a hazard, was built by Deputy Governor John Greene Jr. and his son, Job, shortly after King Philip's War. The house was purchased from the last of the Greene family owners by William Davis Cole in 1817. For many years, it was known as Cole's Farm.

1692 to inquire about establishing a post office and helped bring about the development of a Post Road, which ran from Boston, to Pawtuxet and Apponaug, and eventually to Virginia.

Major Greene is also regarded as a champion for Rhode Island rights and especially as the man who introduced Rhode Island to the controversial practice of using privateers. As England was at war for many years in the 1690–1763 period, there was a demand that merchant ships arm themselves to make war on the mother country's enemies. As an incentive, ships receiving privateer commissions were allowed to keep 9/10ths of the spoils of war. Governor John Easton, fearing that pirates would gain from this practice, hesitated to grant commissions. Deputy Governor Greene had no such reservations and granted commissions, thereby paving the way for a dramatic increase in Rhode Island's commerce.

Warwick's inclination for the sea became obvious quite early. Low prices for agricultural products and the difficulty of acquiring and clearing land made it easy for young men to be lured from their farms to seek adventure and high profits as privateersmen. Historians such as Samuel Greene Arnold have credited Rhode Islanders' vessels with "superior sailing qualities" and Arnold goes on to say, "very few of the enemy's privateers, in a gale of wind, will run or outsail one of our loaded vessels." According to Arnold, 84 vessels of all sizes were built in the colony and were manned by native seamen. A number of these ships were built in the shipyards at Apponaug and Pawtuxet.

The role played by privateers, with all the excitement, however, was only one of the segments of the lucrative maritime enterprises that were to aid in Warwick's growth as a seaport town. In 1712, many of the restrictions placed upon the American colonies in regard to the slave trade were removed. When the Treaty of Utrecht, 1713, which concluded Queen Anne's War, gave England the right to furnish Spanish America with 144,000 slaves over a 30-year period, the colonies were now encouraged to participate in this lucrative trade. Warwick, as well as Rhode Island's other seacoast towns, prospered and became more dependent upon the sea for her prosperity. When there were attempts to curtail the slave trade, Warwick, Newport, and Providence resorted to smuggling.

The key to the maritime prosperity was the trade with the West Indies, which brought sugar and molasses into the colony. This was distilled into rum, a commodity accepted nearly everywhere, and by no means confined to the African trade. The distilling of rum reached a high point in the middle years of the eighteenth century. While Newport, with its 22 distilleries, and Providence, with 12, led the production of rum in the colonies, Warwick also had its share as Pawtuxet's "Stillhouse Cove" implies. At its height, many Rhode Island distilleries could produce rum for about 20¢ per gallon. Approximately 200 gallons, or $40 worth of rum, could purchase a slave in Africa, which, in mid-century, often could be sold for nearly $400 in Cuba or in the Carolinas.

During the first 30 years of the eighteenth century, Warwick's population increased dramatically. It more than doubled from 480 in 1708 to 1,178 in 1730. As the population grew, so did the demand for internal improvements on roads and bridges. As late as 1704, there was no bridge across the Pawtuxet River leading into Warwick. The crossing was at a ford, or "Indian wading place," a short distance below the Pawtuxet side of the present-day Warwick Avenue Bridge.

The Greene homestead at Potowomet was built in the late seventeenth century and greatly altered in the nineteenth century. It remains in the Greene family to the present time. Its owner, Thomas Casey Greene Jr., is shown in front.

Once wagons and other wheeled vehicles came into greater use, serious problems arose, as there were times following excessive rains when the water reached such a height that to ford it was impractical. Between 1704 and 1711, three bridges were built over the Pawtuxet. The first one was built in the Pontiac section of Warwick. It was known as "the great bridge near the Weir," as there was a fish weir or dam at the rapids there. This was then called "Captain Benjamin Greene's bridge" and later "Arnold's bridge." The section was called Clarkesville for many years and eventually became Pontiac. On May 2, 1711, it was felt that a bridge should be built leading into the village of Pawtuxet.

Even as bridges and roads were being built, it was still obvious that the area away from the coast continued to be an unsettled wilderness, with wolves and bears a very real danger. In 1702–03, the bounty on wolves was raised to 20 shillings a head. This was considered a relatively large sum, as a bushel of wheat was 4 shillings, barley was 2, and a pound of wool was 9 pence. Even with such bounties, the dangerous animals were not eliminated until later in the century.

The emphasis on exterminating wolves and other "pests" clearly indicates the importance of agriculture and land in Warwick's eighteenth-century history. Farms were often in the possession of one family for generations. While farming was not the sole occupation of the inhabitants, it was very important and it was often carried out on a subsistence level.

Because of the rocky soil, much of the land was kept as pasture for cattle. Small tracts were cultivated and planted with beans, corn, squash, and other vegetables for family use. Nearly every family raised cows for milk, sheep for wool, and hogs for meat. The wool was spun and woven into cloth, and milk was turned into cheese and butter. Tobacco and cider, as well as surplus amounts of cheese, butter, hams, and wool, were used for trade.

While the West Indies trade brought prosperity, it also brought danger and tragedy. In 1721, smallpox was brought into Massachusetts via ships engaged in the West Indies trade. Before the epidemic subsided, nearly 6,000 cases were reported and 844 deaths resulted. Rhode Island required all goods brought in from Massachusetts to be aired and cleansed and all vessels from infected ports to be quarantined. Anyone coming in from Massachusetts was detained five days along the borders before being allowed into Rhode Island.

Almost from the beginning of the century, Rhode Island won a reputation for contrariness as well as for illegal trading and piracy. This increased after 1733, when the tax called the Molasses Act was passed. The trade in rum, made from molasses, was so lucrative that Warwick ship captains and owners, like most of the others in New England, found it more profitable to smuggle than to comply with the law. The many coves and inlets in Warwick, especially those around Warwick Cove, Mill Pond Cove, and Pawtuxet, made smuggling relatively easy.

England's preoccupation with European wars had a positive effect on Warwick's prosperity, as it was impossible for the mother country to strictly administer the restrictive trade laws or to closely supervise the granting of privileges to privateers. This era in the eighteenth century is often called the "Period of Salutary Neglect," for as England "neglected" her colonies, they prospered, especially in the West Indian trade and in the spoils brought in by the privateers.

Nearly all of Warwick's inhabitants benefited from the increased trade. Those directly concerned with ships and supplies were obvious beneficiaries. In addition, farmers received higher prices, and artisans found a market for their talents as Warwick began supplying the major ports of Newport and Providence. Goods were shipped via a ferry that ran between Warwick Neck and the northern end of Prudence Island and from there to Newport. By 1742, Warwick Neck was a vital link in the postal and commercial trade, as a ferry from Providence stopped there and then sailed on to the islands.

The increased trade created a greater demand for agricultural products and timber. Sawmills and gristmills at Mill Creek, Tuskatucket Brook, Apponaug, and Potowomut were joined by others farther westward until so many farmers settled in the westernmost area of Warwick that, by 1741, it was necessary to divide Warwick to create the Town of Coventry. Over 60 square miles was set aside for the new town and the original town of Warwick was reduced to 43 and 1/10th square miles.

Once Coventry became a separate entity, Warwick turned increasingly toward maritime trade. During the later part of the eighteenth century, Pawtuxet and Apponaug became very active and significant ports in Narragansett Bay. By this period, more ships were leaving Warwick for far-flung ports as the triangular trade between Rhode Island, the West Indies, and Africa increased. Historian S.G. Arnold tells us that during the early part of the century, "The classes of vessels built were ships, brigantines and sloops." Warwick shipyards, which existed as early as 1690, turned out a number of sloops and brigantines.

The distilling of rum was another important aspect of life in Warwick. The operation of a stillhouse had its own peculiar problems, and the story of the death of Dr. Zuriel Waterman attests to it. George Waterman made the following statement on September 20, 1786:

> Joseph Rhodes Senior descended a Cistern in the distill House to discharge a quantity of Putrid stagnated water; . . . as soon as he arrived to the bottom, he [said] "how dreadfully it smells here, I feel faint!" . . . he fell immediately.

Zachariah Rhodes and Zuriel Waterman went into the vat to help the stricken man, and they were both overcome by the fumes. Zachariah survived, but Joseph Rhodes and Zuriel Waterman suffocated.

There were also great profits and dangers involved in the use of rum to purchase African natives for the nefarious slave trade. One house that is still standing as a reminder of the part Warwick captains played in this trade is the Captain Thomas Remington house at 47–49 Post Road in the Pawtuxet section of Warwick. Many old-time Pawtuxet residents attest that they can remember when there were still chains and shackles in the basement of the old 1740 Colonial house. It is a general belief that the captain quartered his chained slaves in a small building behind the house and held slave auctions in his barn. A number of similar stories have been told concerning the Moses Greene house, located at the Mill Cove in Old Warwick.

The maritime activities of Warwick's sailors were not confined to the triangular trade exclusively, for there was also fishing, whaling, and the coastal trade. Without doubt, however, the lucrative profits made from the triangular trade dominated, and any attempt

Governor William Greene (1743–1758) lived in the lovely home near Division Street in Warwick. He was in office during the struggles for power between the English and the French. His son was also governor of Rhode Island, during the Revolutionary War. This portrait was painted by Peter Pelham (1684–1751).

by England to curtail the trade with the West Indies resulted in opposition. Warwick, with its coves and inlets, joined the rest of the colony in smuggling activities after the mother country passed the 1708 Acts of Trade and the 1733 Molasses Act, which placed taxes on goods coming in from the West Indies that would diminish the colonists' profit. This defiance of the trade acts continued almost unabated until 1754, when the "Old French War" began. This war, known in America as the French and Indian War, lasted until 1763. At the beginning of this conflict, William Greene of Warwick was the governor of the colony and its key political figure.

The French and Indian War witnessed the colony engaging in illegal trade with the enemy. An embargo had been passed on trade with the West Indies, but Rhode Island repeatedly violated this and continued to trade with the French and Spanish colonies. It was during this war that a large number of Warwick men sailed on privateers. Historian S.G. Arnold estimated that by 1759, one-fifth of the adult male population in Rhode Island was "at this time engaged on board of private armed ships." While the profits were great, so, too, were the dangers. Over 130 ships from Narragansett ports were "taken, plundered, cast away, and lost at sea" from 1756 to 1763 and many Warwick sailors were aboard them.

Natural calamities also had its effect on the town. In February 1759, a great flood caused a considerable amount of damage in Warwick. The south end of the Pawtuxet Bridge was nearly destroyed. In addition, Warwick witnessed two earthquake shocks in the spring and a major nor'easter storm in the winter of 1761. It was during 1761–62 that so many disastrous fires occurred that the colony's old fire laws were amended to read as follows:

> each dwelling-house should be furnished with a leathern bucket, having the
> owner's name painted upon it, and a ladder to reach to the top of the house, or
> in lieu thereof, a trap door in the roof.

By February 1763, the French and Indian War was over. The Peace of Paris was signed, ending what historians have called "the most wide-spread, costly, and sanguinary strife which the world had ever seen." Within a short time, the cost of the war and the fruits of the victory proved to be the wedge that would separate the American colonists from England. Warwick played a significant role in this struggle.

This home, located on Love Lane and Division Streets and built by Samuel Gorton Jr., served as the residence for two Rhode Island governors: William Greene Sr. and William Greene Jr. The house was also visited by many important Revolutionary War figures, such as Benjamin Franklin and Nathanael Greene.

3. THE REVOLUTIONARY ERA

The conclusion of hostilities between the British and her adversaries in 1763 brought discord to Warwick as the mother country sought to use the colonies to pay for the cost of the war. Warwick, much like other seacoast towns, believed that England, in her zeal to enforce her laws, threatened to destroy colonial trade and usurped the colonists' rights as Englishmen.

While Newport was the scene of a number of minor acts of violence against the British crown, it was in Warwick that the most serious of the early protests against the British took place. This was the burning of British revenue schooner the *Gaspee* in June 1772 off Namquit Point in Warwick.

Relations between the British patrols in Narragansett Bay and the colonists had reached a new low point after 1763, when British Admiral Montagu selected Lieutenant William Dudingston, captain of the *Gaspee*, to patrol the waters of Narragansett Bay. An incident involving Dudingston and Nathanael Greene, who was to become Rhode Island's most celebrated Revolutionary War hero, eventually led to the first act of violence in the Revolution when the *Gaspee* was burned.

On February 17, 1772, the small vessel *Fortune*, under the command of Rufus Greene, an East Greenwich cousin of Nathanael Greene, was anchored in a North Kingstown harbor. Under normal conditions, neither the sloop nor the cargo was large enough to warrant much attention from a revenue schooner, especially while in port. Dudingston was no ordinary British officer, however, and seemed to enjoy harassing any and all vessels, especially those owned by some of Rhode Island's most influential families. Once the schooner *Gaspee* reached the *Fortune*, Dudingston sent one of his officers, a man named Dundas, to board the Greenes' ship.

Captain Rufus Greene, then 23 years old and well schooled in the trading fraternity of New England, asked "by what authority?" Captain Greene reported that when he realized the boarding party from the *Gaspee* had lifted the *Fortune*'s anchor, he went forward to stop them, believing that the British had no right to seize his ship. Dundas reacted harshly. Greene was knocked down, confined to his cabin for a time, and then forced to board the *Gaspee*. The *Fortune* was then towed to Newport and shortly after sent to Boston. This clearly violated one of the King's statutes, which required cases such as this to be tried in the Admiralty Court of Rhode Island. Nathanael Greene and his brothers, as owners of the *Fortune*, quickly brought a suit against Dudingston.

In order to do this, the Greenes hired the very brilliant East Greenwich attorney James M. Varnum. As a result, a deep friendship grew between Varnum and Nathanael Greene, which eventually resulted in the formation of the Kentish Guards. Because this business took Greene to East Greenwich for much of the time, he stayed at the home of his cousin, William Greene, and there met Catherine Littlefield, his future wife.

To avoid being served with the writ prepared by Varnum on behalf of the Greenes, Dudingston stayed aboard his ship, the *Gaspee*, for nearly three months and continued to harass small sloops in Narragansett Bay. Charles Carroll, in his *Rhode Island: Three Centuries of Democracy*, writes that "The day of reckoning for Dudingston and the *Gaspee* came early in June." On June 8, 1772, Providence sloop *Hannah*, owned by John Brown and under the captaincy of Benjamin Lindsey, left Newport harbor for Providence. She was approached by the *Gaspee*, which attempted to overhaul her.

Captain Lindsey had no intention of submitting to search while it was possible to outwit Dudingston and outsail the *Gaspee*. Lindsey quickly began to outrun the larger British vessel. Besides the advantage of speed, the Providence vessel was of a "lighter draft" and could sail in shallow water. Lindsey realized that the *Gaspee* was recklessly chasing him, and at Namquit Point, since known as Gaspee Point, Captain Lindsey turned the *Hannah* sharply to the west, seemingly to elude the *Gaspee*. Lindsey warily avoided shoal water and lured the larger vessel into a sand bar, where she ran hard aground.

Fortunately, Ephraim Bowen, who later became one of Warwick's leading citizens and who took part in the burning of the *Gaspee*, gave an eyewitness account of the events that took place during that historic action. Bowen did not write of the stirring events, however, until August 1839, when over 67 years had passed. Bowen, despite his 86 years of age, had excellent recall and his story, sharpened by frequent repetition, is accurate in almost every detail.

According to Bowen, Lindsey "arrived at Providence about sunset, when he immediately informed Mr. John Brown, one of our first and most respectable merchants of the situation of the *Gaspee* . . ." Brown quickly realized this was an opportunity to destroy the British revenue schooner and issued a call for all who wished to join him in the move against the *Gaspee*.

Most historians believe that no disguises were worn and that John Brown was a member of the party. While there is no evidence in Bowen's account that any men from Warwick were in the party, Horace Belcher believed, "there is good evidence that a least one boat came from Pawtuxet." Captain Abraham Whipple, who led the party, carefully approached the *Gaspee* "bow on bow" to avoid a broadside from the batteries of the British vessel. Dudingston was summoned on deck by his sentries and asked the approaching ship, "Who comes there?" Captain Whipple is said to have answered, "I want to come on Board." Dudingston said, "Stand off, you can't come on board." Whipple then is alleged to have said words to the effect, "I am the sheriff of the county of Kent. I am come for the commander of this vessel, and have him I will, dead or alive; men, spring to your oars!"

Bowen, in his narrative says, "As soon as Dudingston began to hail, Joseph Bucklin, who was standing by the main thwart, by my right side, said to me, 'Eph, reach me your gun, and I can kill that fellow." Bowen remembered, "I reached it to him, accordingly; when, during Capt. Whipple's replying, Bucklin fired and Dudingston fell; and Bucklin exclaimed, 'I have killed the rascal.' " Soon after Captain Whipple's answer, the boats were alongside the British revenue schooner and boarded her without opposition.

Dudingston fell to the deck with wounds in the groin and arm. Both Ephraim Bowen and Dr. John Mawney, who also participated in the event, gave excellent accounts of the action on that fateful day. As a trained medical man, Mawney hastened to the cabin and tended to Dudingston's wounds. Shortly after Dudingston was cared for, the crew of the *Gaspee* was taken from the vessel. Bowen, who was very familiar with Pawtuxet recalled that they "landed Dudingston at the old Stillhouse Wharf at Pawtuxet, and put the chief into the house of Joseph Rhodes."

Dudingston, perhaps because Whipple claimed to be "the sheriff of the county of Kent," firmly believed that Nathanael Greene was in charge of the raiding party. Greene, in a letter to Samuel Ward Jr., dated January 25, 1773, makes it clear that he was not present at the *Gaspee*'s burning.

The significance of the defiance of Rhode Islanders in 1772 extended beyond the isolated incident of June 9. The news of the burning spread from Rhode Island to the rest of the colonies. Many openly applauded this "first act of violence" and made preparations for assistance should the British react with force. Committees of Correspondence, the forerunner of the Continental Congress, were organized as a result. Recognizing the

One of the most significant acts in Warwick's history was that of the burning of the British revenue schooner Gaspee *on June 9, 1772. (Courtesy artist Karl Doerflinger.)*

significance of the event, Warwick's Namquit Point became known as the place where the *Gaspee* was burned and, in time, became known as Gaspee Point.

In his 1875 *History of Warwick*, O.P. Fuller notes, "Though the town of Warwick was no more interested in or affected by the war of the Revolution than some of the other towns of the State, it happily fell to its lot to furnish several men who became conspicuous during the time, both in the councils of State and in the field." Among the many outstanding leaders from Warwick's families who served with great distinction on both land and sea were Major General Nathanael Greene, Colonel Christopher Greene, Lieutenant Colonel Christopher Lippitt, Colonel John Waterman, Captain Samuel Aborn, Captain Robert Rhodes, and Governor William Greene Jr.

In 1774, as the fear of war began to make itself felt, Nathanael Greene and his friend, James Mitchell Varnum, along with a number of young men from East Greenwich, Coventry, and Warwick, began to make preparations for the formation of a military company. The Military Independent Company, or "cadets," as the members called themselves, met regularly at the home of William Arnold in East Greenwich. This company was the forerunner of the Kentish Guards, which received widespread acclaim and praise during the early years of the Revolutionary War.

In September 1774, Nathanael Greene made a clandestine trip to Boston to purchase a musket and returned with a "deserter" from the British army. It is generally believed that the "deserter" was William Johnson, who agreed to teach the cadets military drill and tactics. In October, a petition drawn up by James M. Varnum requested that the military company be chartered and incorporated under the name "Kentish Guards."

Warwick's annual Gaspee Day Parade attracts many thousands of spectators and a large number of colonial militia units. The beginning of the parade is signaled by a volley fired from the Newport Artillery Revolutionary War cannon.

Christopher Greene, one of Warwick's great heroes, joined the Kentish Guards in 1774, took part in the ill-fated attempt to conquer Canada, and made a heroic stand at Red Bank in New Jersey.

In addition to the Warwick men who joined the Kentish Guards were the men who formed the Pawtuxet Rangers. The men of Pawtuxet, on October 29, 1774, obtained a charter from the Rhode Island Assembly and organized the Pawtuxet Rangers. For their captain, the militiamen elected Samuel Aborn, who two years earlier, in his small sloop *Sally* had taken the anchors, guns, stores, and other effects from the *Gaspee* to Pawtuxet. Benjamin Arnold and Rhodes Arnold were lieutenants in the Rangers, and Stephen Greene was elected to the position of ensign. Horace Belcher noted that "At least half the membership bore the family names Aborn, Arnold, Rhodes, and Smith."

Both the Pawtuxet Rangers and the Kentish Guards became significant Colonial military units in the Revolutionary War. The Kentish Guards selected James M. Varnum to be their first leader as they proceeded to drill and prepare for resistance to British tyranny.

This remarkable military unit, which contained a number of members of the Greene family, eventually furnished two generals for the Continental army (Nathanael Greene and James M. Varnum), and at least three colonels, one of whom was Colonel Christopher Greene. This cousin and friend of Nathanael was the hero of the ill-fated venture to Quebec and of the Battle of Red Bank in New Jersey. The Guards also supplied the state and the country with a number of very capable lieutenant colonels, majors, captains, and lieutenants.

Ironically, the services of Nathanael Greene were almost lost at this point. The Guards, after a vote in East Greenwich, rejected Nathanael Greene as an officer because he walked with a slight limp. Varnum was so incensed with the vote that he seriously contemplated

General Nathanael Greene, seen here in a portrait by Charles Wilson Peale, played a key part in America's success story during the Revolutionary War.

leaving the group. Greene, however, swallowed his pride and asked Varnum not to resign. Neither Varnum nor Greene resigned, and Greene remained in the ranks as a private. The Guards drilled for three days a week under the guidance of William Johnson and Greene never missed a meeting. When the news reached Warwick of the bloodshed at Lexington and Concord on April 19, 1775, both Greene and the Kentish Guards were ready to make their mark in history.

On April 22, 1775, the Rhode Island Legislature met at Providence and called for an "army of observation, . . . properly armed and disciplined, . . . to repel any insult or violence that may be offered to the inhabitants." Governor Joseph Wanton, who had just been reelected, and Deputy Governor Darius Sessions opposed the action. As a result, the legislature refused to give Wanton the oath of office and replaced him with Deputy Governor Nicholas Cooke.

The legislature met again on May 3 and called for an army of 1,500 men to be formed into one brigade of three regiments. The regiments were to be recruited in Newport and Bristol Counties under Colonel Thomas Church, in Providence County under Colonel Daniel Hitchcock, and in Kent and Kings Counties under Colonel James M. Varnum. Recruitment to join these regiments was encouraged with a promise of a bounty of $4 to those who agreed to join for a six-month period.

Victory and independence did not come easily. The eight long years between the outbreak of hostilities in 1775 to the final victory in 1783 meant a great deal of suffering and hardship for Warwick. With the exception of three battles, Rhode Island troops fought in every major action of the war.

On May 8, 1775, to the continued amazement of historians, the legislature sent a letter to Nathanael Greene informing him of his command. Why Nathanael Greene, a private at this time, was selected to lead the troops has never been fully answered. Richard K. Showman in his foreword to *The Papers of General Nathanael Greene*, cites Greene's political connections, which included Samuel Ward, one of Rhode Island's members to the Continental Congress, as a possible reason and adds, "There were men with military experience, however, who had even better political connections with the dominant Hopkins faction." Showman concludes by saying, "Perhaps by some miracle the leaders of the Rhode Island Assembly recognized his hidden genius; it is more likely that like the winner of a lottery they simply picked the right number."

Greene immediately proceeded to his new tasks as brigadier general with the same zeal and enthusiasm that marked all his endeavors. After conferring with authorities in Providence, he proceeded to Cambridge, Massachusetts, and he and his troops soon became involved in the siege of Boston.

It was during this period that a number of Warwick men, including Christopher Greene, became participants in the invasion of Canada. George Washington, believing that American success depended upon the capture of Montreal and Quebec, envisioned a two-prong attack in 1775. He ordered General Benedict Arnold, with 1,000 volunteers, to invade through Maine and attack Quebec. Christopher Greene, a kinsman of Nathanael, who was a major in Varnum's regiment at the time, was promoted to lead one of the two battalions. Three of the companies under Lieutenant Colonel Greene were commanded by Rhode Islanders: Samuel Ward Jr., John Topham, and Simeon Thayer. Unfortunately, the expedition proved to be one of the most grueling and unsuccessful campaigns of the war.

After a number of delays, the American attack was launched on December 31, 1775. Simeon Thayer, one of the three Rhode Islanders captains in Lieutenant Colonel Greene's battalion, fortunately kept a diary of the events that followed. The attack was made in a "prodigious snowstorm" and was successful at the onset. American troops, led by Christopher Greene, entered the city and victory seemed within their grasp. Elsewhere on the battlefield, however, the Americans met with stunning reversals, and General Arnold had no alternative but to call for a retreat. The Rhode Island forces within the city found themselves trapped and had no choice but to accept the relatively good terms the British offered.

In time, the prisoners were freed and many, including Christopher Greene and Samuel Ward Jr., returned to join their regiments and play an important role in the outcome of the war. Colonel Christopher Greene especially felt the sting of failure and vowed never to surrender again.

In 1775, the British naval commander in Narragansett Bay, Captain James Wallace, brought fear to the hearts of the residents of Warwick and Providence. Wallace threatened an attack on Providence and sent a fleet to the upper part of Narragansett Bay. He stopped near Conimicut Point and pillaged the area around Warwick Neck, stealing a large number of livestock. Shortly after this, in October, Wallace ordered the bombardment of Bristol.

According to Edward Field's *Revolutionary Defences of R.I.*, "Following this affair at Bristol, the works at Kettle Point and Pawtuxet were thrown up, batteries were located all along the seaboard, and permanent guards were established." The fort in Pawtuxet was known during this early period as Fort Cranston Neck, Fort Pawtuxet Neck, and eventually Fort Neck. It was built on land owned by Captain Thomas Remington and was hastily manned with a company of 50 men.

At that time, it was believed the enemy would attack Warwick Neck and there was a great deal of concentration on that area. A little over a year later, General Francois de Malmedy, a French officer appointed to direct the operation of Rhode Island forts, placed the emphasis on Fort Neck in Pawtuxet rather than at Warwick Neck.

In December 1775, the Continental Congress created a Continental Navy, and Rhode Islander Esek Hopkins was appointed as commander-in-chief. A number of seamen familiar with Warwick ports were given commands. Among these, Abraham Whipple and John B. Hopkins were named as captains and Rhodes Arnold was commissioned as a first lieutenant.

For a short while in the spring of 1776, the calamities of war seemed to be balanced by good fortune in Rhode Island. It was not uncommon in many Warwick families to see father and son, uncles, and even grandfathers taking some part in the military actions of the period. In Pawtuxet and Warwick, this was especially true of the Greene, Arnold, and Rhodes families. As nearly all Warwick men had some experience with the sea, many volunteered to serve with Whipple and Hopkins in the fledgling Continental Navy. A great deal of optimism during the early period of the war came when word reached Rhode Island that Esek Hopkins was in New London after a successful voyage as commander of

Seen here in Narragansett Bay, this beautiful replica is one of Rhode Island's most famous Revolutionary War vessels, the Providence. *As the* Katy, *it was the first ship in the Rhode Island Navy, rechristened the* Providence, *and served as one of the original vessels in the Continental Navy.*

The Pawtuxet Rangers Militia Unit was chartered in October 1774. During the Revolution, it protected the village by manning the fort at Pawtuxet Neck and participating in the Battle of Rhode Island. Now, they are the host unit for the Gaspee Day Parade.

the Continental Navy. Fort Nassau in the Bahamas had been captured, and the fleet returned with much needed supplies.

Many Warwick and Rhode Island men, however, preferred the more lucrative service of "privateering" than service in the Continental Navy. This method of warfare, regarded by many as legalized piracy, had long been a favored enterprise in the colony. In March 1776, privateering, which is the issuance of letters of marque and reprisal, was legalized in Rhode Island in conformity with an act of the Continental Congress. As might be expected, the wealthy maritime families of Rhode Island took part in this venture. John Brown of Providence became famous, if not notorious, for his part, and Warwick's Greene, Rhodes, and Aborn families played leading roles.

While Rhode Island was busily engaged in building defences and celebrating the victories of Esek Hopkins's voyage to Nassau, the bay was temporarily free of British ships. Realizing this, Rhode Island chose this time to issue what is generally regarded as the Rhode Island Declaration of Independence on May 4, 1776. This came two months before the general Declaration of the United Colonies. The Rhode Island document was written by Dr. Jonathan Arnold and signed by Governor Nicholas Cooke and the deputies from the various towns. William Greene, Jacob Greene, Charles Holden Jr., and John Waterman were the deputies from Warwick who signed this May 4 act of independence.

At the time that Rhode Island passed her May 4 renunciation of the King, those Warwick soldiers who had joined the Continental Army were with Nathanael Greene in New York. Greene's major problems during this early period were keeping his troops working on the fortifications and keeping the men in camp. Many American soldiers, away from home for the first time, found the large city of New York a most powerful attraction.

A Pawtuxet Ranger officer, Lieutenant Ronald Barnes, puts a class of seniors from CCRI through the drill of loading and firing a Revolutionary War cannon.

By June, however, the reality of the seriousness and difficulties of war superseded all other problems. In July, Greene began to complain that "a putrid fever prevailed in my brigade." This sickness spread rapidly through the troops and to other parts of the camp. General Greene was also stricken with the fever and, as a result, was out of action for a period of time.

At home in Warwick, the fear of smallpox, "putrid fever," and other diseases was accompanied by a fear of invasion. As early as January 1776, the General Assembly ordered "that a number of men not exceeding fifty, be stationed at Warwick Neck, including the Artillery Company in Warwick; the remainder to be minutemen; that Col. John Waterman have the command . . ."

Not long after, according to historian Edward Field, "A watch-house was ordered to be built on . . . Pawtuxet Neck." This fort was "twelve feet long and eight feet wide, for the accommodations of the guard stationed at the fort." This early fort had a battery of two 18-pound guns and was placed under the command of Colonel Samuel Aborn and "for a great part of the time was garrisoned by the Pawtuxet Rangers."

During the summer and fall of 1776, when Pawtuxet and Warwick men were actively fighting the British to obtain independence, much of the difficult work of keeping the colony alive was left to the women. Benjamin Cowell, writing in 1850, commented on the following in his *Spirit of '76 in Rhode Island*: "From December, 1776, to the summer of 1777, almost every man liable by law, or not liable, to perform military duty, was called out to guard the shores . . ." With relatively few exceptions, the women often found themselves without male help and faced the rigors of war and everyday life alone. Cowell stated that "Night and day incursions were made from the ships-towns near the shore were bombarded and burnt . . . spies would furnish the necessary information where there was a herd of cattle or a flock of sheep, and in many cases act as guides to the enemy in their marauding excursions."

Cowell interviewed a number of women in an effort to help them receive Revolutionary War pensions and recounted stories of women who during "hay time" went into the meadow, "pillowed her baby on some hay in the shade, and went to work." While some "knit stockings for the whole guard," others "raked and loaded hay, hoed and gathered in potatoes, harvested corn . . . and did . . . whatever her husband would have done had he been at home . . ."

Anna Aldrich, one of the women interviewed by Cowell, told that in order to do this work, she cradled her baby "in the boughs of a tree, secured in a blanket from reptiles— so that literally, in the words of an old nursery song, 'When the wind blew, the cradle would rock.' "

Many of these women never saw their men return home, as the fortunes of war in the summer and fall of 1776 turned against the American cause. Rhode Island Continentals in New York, for the first time, met the enemy face to face and endured a devastating defeat at Long Island. The sad state of affairs in New Jersey and New York, in the eyes of most Rhode Islanders, was matched by the turn of events in Narragansett Bay. On December 3, the British entered Rhode Island waters with 7 ships of the line, 4 frigates, and 70 transports with 6,000 troops aboard.

The destination for the British fleet was Newport. On December 8, 1776, the King's army landed in Middletown, and historian S.G. Arnold noted, "after a night of pillage, the next morning marched into Newport." Within a few days, officials in neighboring Massachusetts and Connecticut, realizing the danger to the mainland of Rhode Island and to their states, sent help to contain the British in Newport. S.G. Arnold writes that "These men were quartered at all the defensible points on each side of the bay. The State and the island were two great and hostile camps." Some of these neighboring troops were assigned to defend the fort at Pawtuxet Neck.

A brigade, consisting of three regiments, was created for a 15-month enlistment to defend the state. James M. Varnum, who had resigned his position as colonel in the Continental Army, was appointed as brigadier general.

General Washington, in desperate need of a victory to bolster morale, made the decision to attack the Hessian troops under Colonel Johann Rails at Trenton, New Jersey. Washington's army, by this time, was reduced to less than 6,000 effective troops, and this number would be greatly reduced on December 31, when enlistments would expire. On Christmas Eve, Washington and his staff met at General Nathanael Greene's headquarters in the Merrick house near the banks of the Delaware River. On the following day, one of the most dramatic and significant battles of the Revolutionary War was fought. Many historians, greatly impressed with this early victory, have written volumes on how Washington's men crossed the half-frozen Delaware River and surprised the well-trained, highly disciplined Hessians as they were "still sleeping off their Christmas celebrations." Despite almost insurmountable difficulties, the Americans were successful.

The fort at Pawtuxet was manned by the Pawtuxet Rangers, officially ranked in the state militia as the Second Independent Company of the County of Kent, which at that time numbered 50 and were led by Captain Samuel Aborn, First Lieutenant Benjamin Arnold, Second Lieutenant Rhodes Arnold, and Ensign Stephen Greene. The commander of the militia unit was Samuel Aborn, one of the leading citizens of the village and the "host at the Golden Ball Inn, on Post Road, at the western end of the village." Aborn remained the Rangers' commander throughout the struggle for independence.

His experiences during the war serve to remind today's generations of the bitterness and the tragedy of the time. Very early in the struggle, his sloop *Sally* was captured by the British, causing him serious financial hardship. Later, his young son, a boy of 14, joined the Continental Army. Boys at that young age were anxious to take part in the war and often served as drummer-boys. Young Aborn, at the special request of General Nathanael Greene, was granted permission to return home because of ill health. Horace Belcher noted that it was too late as "the boy came home only to die."

The fort, with its small watch house, became the responsibility of the Rangers, who not only took part in building it, but also manned it during the early months of 1777. The Rangers at this time were more than armed villagers, as each man furnished his own musket and equipment. Officers studied military drill and tactics and provided additional supplies and equipment. Most of the Rangers carried out their business in the village, subject to call when needed.

The Pawtuxet Rangers were relieved of their duty at Fort Neck in April 1777 by the Providence Company of Cadets, commanded by Colonel Joseph Nightingale. The Rangers resumed their duty in May, and for the duration of the war manned the fort. On a number of occasions, other units relieved them briefly, while the principal responsibility of the fort rested with the Rangers.

In February, with General Washington's consent, two continental battalions were raised by the state. Warwick's Colonel Christopher Greene, while still a prisoner of the British, was selected to head the first battalion with Samuel Ward Jr. as its major. Israel Angell of Providence was appointed to command the second battalion. Before the war's end, all of these men would rank high as the state's leading patriots.

Real estate value in Warwick sank at least 25 percent in value, and according to W.A. Greene, "since the blockade it had cost the inhabitants to live, on an average, three shillings per week more than their earnings . . . Corn cost $20 per bushel; rye $25 per bushel . . ."

Reports of the sad condition of Rhode Island troops in the Continental Army further demoralized the state. According to S.G. Arnold's history of the state, "Col. Angell described his soldiers as being without shoes, and otherwise so poorly clad, that half were unfit for any duty, and the regiment had become an object of derision wherever it appeared." Despair and fear among the troops increased, and a near mutiny broke out in Colonel Christopher Greene's battalion. General James M. Varnum was called upon to suppress the action and, fortunately, was able to quiet the troops and avert any drastic consequences.

It was in the midst of this suffering and dissatisfaction that Rhode Island's Major William Barton led a group of men into one of the most daring and thrilling accomplishments of the Revolutionary War. The feat was the capture of a British general from the island at a time when the enemy forces were very strong and seemingly

Captain Oliver Gardiner, who built this house in 1750, took an active part in the Revolutionary War. He was in command of the "Row Galley," which harassed the British in Narragansett Bay. The house still stands on Post Road in Cowesett.

infallible. Barton, a young officer from Warren, heard of the abuses by General Richard Prescott, the British officer in command of Newport. Barton also received information that General Prescott often visited the Overing house, a lovely home about 5 miles north of Newport. Common gossip among British soldiers in Newport taverns alleged that Prescott only visited the home after sending the Tory, Overing, on a long trade mission and that the object of his visit was to be with Mrs. Overing.

To surprise the British, Barton decided to launch his attack from Warwick. He selected 40 men he believed most proficient in the handling of boats and on July 7, the Barton crew, under cover of darkness, rowed across the bay to Warwick Neck. Here, they hid their shallow vessels in the bushes for fear the enemy might notice the unusual number of boats at the neck. After being delayed by a storm, Barton's daring crew left Warwick and, with muffled oars, proceeded across the bay. Colonel John Waterman, commander of the garrison at the fort on Warwick Neck, agreed to post a sharp lookout in the event the British should discover the expedition and attempt to cut Barton off from reaching the mainland. In that case, the Warwick men agreed to leave the safety of Warwick Neck and row to the north end of Prudence Island to rescue Barton and his troops.

A number of British ships were stationed along the eastern end of Prudence Island and Barton's whale boats rowed by so close they could hear the sentinels cry of "All's well." The men landed on the shore, about a mile from the Overing house, where Prescott was staying as a guest of Mrs. Overing. They quickly overpowered a lone sentry and then

The David Arnold Tavern, built in 1750 on the old Apponaug-Old Warwick Road (West Shore Road), was the location where Colonel Barton took the captured British general Richard Prescott.

burst into Prescott's room and captured him. Prescott was allowed to put on but a few clothes and with his aide and his sentinel, was rushed to the boats.

Once again the Rhode Islanders rowed past the British vessels lying at anchor, and by midnight Barton's men and their prisoners were back at Warwick Neck. The amazing episode, according to S.A. Greene, took but six and one-half hours. Prescott was taken to David Arnold's tavern on West Shore Road. A bewildered Prescott is said to have remarked, "Sir, I did not think it possible you could escape the vigilance of the water guards."

While Warwick enjoyed a brief period of high spirits following Major Barton's capture of the British General Richard Prescott, there was a touch of gloom later in the year with the news of American defeats at Brandywine, Philadelphia, and Germantown.

It was during 1777, called "the time of mixed fortunes" and the "year of miracles," that the British had planned a three-pronged attack to cut the colonies in half along the line of Lake Champlain and the Hudson Valley. Three British armies were to meet at Albany and present an unmatched force that would have devastated the Continental Army. Fortunately for the American cause, poor communications and a series of blunders made this impossible. As a result, only the army under General John Burgoyne met the Americans at Saratoga, not far from Albany.

General Washington had sent many of his best troops to Saratoga to aid General Horatio Gates and his second in command, General Benedict Arnold. In addition, militia units from all over New England, possibly including Warwick, swelled the American ranks. General Burgoyne ordered an attack on the Americans on October 7, 1777. He advanced with 1,500 men and 6 pieces of artillery. The British might have been successful, but Arnold, without orders and in defiance of Gates, whom many believed was about to call for a retreat, pressed to the front and actually took command of the American forces. Led by Arnold, the Continentals turned a near defeat into a resounding victory. Burgoyne found himself surrounded, defeated, and, with no hope of aid from other British forces, compelled to surrender on October 17, 1777.

The village of Pawtuxet maintains a very strong tradition regarding the Battle of Saratoga and has the belief that two cannon and a number of prisoners taken at the famous October 1777 battle came to Pawtuxet. Experts disagree on the participation of the Pawtuxet Rangers in the battle and doubt that the two valuable cannon were taken to the small village.

In addition to the splendid news of the victory at Saratoga, Warwick was thrilled to learn that one of its native sons, Christopher Greene, had made a magnificent defense of Fort Mercer at Red Bank, one of the forts on the Delaware River. Greene had but 400 men and 8 artillerists to defend the strategic fort against the might of the British and Hessians. Count Carl von Donop, desiring to wipe out the loss his Hessian troops had suffered at Trenton on Christmas Day, 1776, asked British General William Howe to allow him the honor of capturing Red Bank. Donop, with 1,200 well-trained Hessian troops, crossed the Delaware late in the afternoon of October 22, 1777, and demanded that Colonel Greene surrender. The reply of Greene to Donop has become a classic response, for, according to S.G. Arnold, Greene replied, "with these brave fellows this fort shall be my tomb."

Shortly after Greene's refusal to surrender, an overconfident Hessian army attacked the fort. They quickly occupied the abandoned position, but as they approached the inner walls, Greene gave the order to fire. The result was devastating as musket and artillery fire quickly decimated the Hessian force. Over 153 Hessians were killed, over 200 gravely wounded, and their commander, Donop, was mortally wounded. In their panic, the Hessians fled, abandoning Donop, who was made a prisoner and died three days later. The American loss was 14 killed and 23 wounded.

This great victory assured Christopher Greene and his Rhode Island troops a high place in the history of the Revolutionary War and made Greene the natural choice for recruiting a regiment of black and Indian slaves in Rhode Island. The concept of a regiment made up of slaves was proposed by General James Mitchell Varnum, and was adopted by the General Assembly on February 9, 1778. The act freed all slaves in Rhode Island who enlisted in the Continental Army and provided that their owners would be paid by the State.

The great American victory at Saratoga, plus the eloquence and persuasive powers of Benjamin Franklin, brought about the long desired Franco-American alliance against the British. When, in 1778, it became obvious that a large French fleet would be sent to America, Rhode Island hopes were high that the British could be driven from Newport. Washington agreed that the time was right to commit Continental Army troops to Rhode Island and selected General John Sullivan to command the campaign against the British on Aquidneck Island.

On July 24, 1778, General Washington decided to send General Nathanael Greene to Rhode Island to aid the expedition. In justifying this to Congress, Washington wrote, "He is intimately acquainted with the whole of the Country, and besides he has extensive interest and influence on it." All seemed to favor the American effort in the early days of August, but soon misunderstandings occurred between the American and French forces that hampered the expedition. Resentments and poor communication made the necessary type of cooperation nearly impossible and resulted in an unfortunate delay.

Word reached Warwick that the date set for the invasion of Aquidneck Island was August 8, 1778. General John Sullivan had at that time an estimated 6,000 troops at his disposal and more militia units were arriving daily. Hoping to greatly strengthen his numbers, Sullivan decided to postpone the invasion until August 12. Unfortunately, one of the area's most devastating hurricanes wreaked havoc at that time with American, French, and British strategies. For two and a half days, the storm raged uninhibited and caused serious damage to both the French and British ships, which had been engaged about 80 miles south of Newport.

The same storm struck the American troops on Aquidneck Island on the evening of August 11, 1778. Richard K. Showman, editor of *The Papers of General Nathanael Greene*, noted, "It tore up tents and leveled the camp, filling trenches, destroying stores, and soaking powder and cartridges to uselessness. Without protection from the wind and rain, the men found sleep impossible. Lacking dry ammunition, the Americans' situation was desperate . . ." Historian S.G. Arnold wrote, "Some of the men died of exposure and a great number of horses perished . . . as a result of the hurricane. Many of the militia were unseasoned in battle and afraid as they believed the storm was a bad omen and some deserted."

Despite these setbacks, the Americans felt victory could be theirs and decided to proceed with the plan. One of the reasons that Sullivan was able to continue the attack was that Governor William Greene had replaced the gunpowder that had been ruined by the hurricane. Sullivan, at 6:00 a.m. on August 15, ordered the American army to move south. When the French fleet left Narragansett Bay to repair the damages received as a result of the hurricane, American forces became demoralized and many deserted.

After careful consideration, the decision was made to fall back to the fortifications near Butt's Hill, on the north end of Aquidneck Island. On August 28, the American army began its strategic retreat with Nathanael Greene leading the troops from the trenches near the British lines. The withdrawal began at 9 p.m. under cover of darkness and by 3 a.m. on the following morning, the entire American army had reached Butt's Hill undetected. It was daybreak before the British commander, General Robert Pigot, learned that the Americans had gone.

As the American troops retreated to the northern end of Aquidneck Island and were preparing to defend themselves from the British, Rhode Islanders on the mainland heard the heavy cannonade at about 9 a.m. Many residents along Warwick's coast went to high hills to try to see what was happening. According to Horace Belcher, "Polly Rhodes, watching through a spy glass from an upper window of a Rhodes house on the Warwick side of Main St . . . [saw] the dark clouds of smoke hovering over the waters of the lower

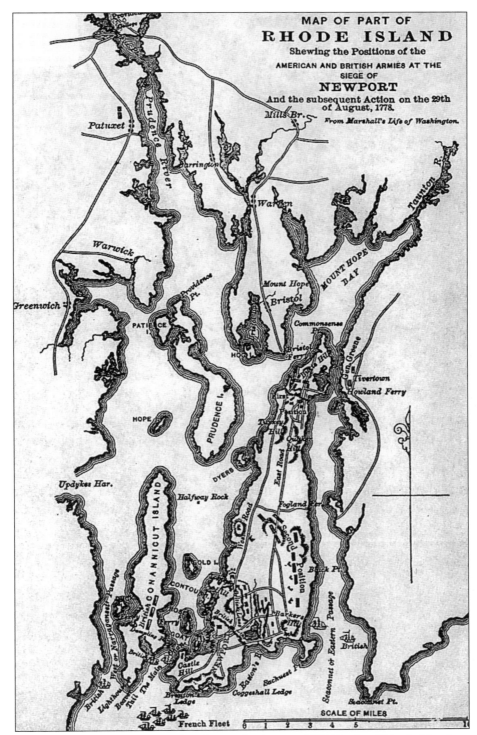

This 1832 map is one of the few that depicts the August 1778 Battle of Rhode Island.

Captain Robert Rhodes, the great-grandson of Pawtuxet's founder, Zachariah Rhodes, was the oldest captain at the Battle of Rhode Island in 1778. (Courtesy the Henry A.L. Brown Collection.)

bay." Her husband, Sylvester Rhodes, and many of her friends and neighbors of the Pawtuxet Rangers were engaged in this classic battle.

It was during this action that Colonel Greene's Black Regiment, under Major Samuel Ward Jr., won everlasting fame. The ex-slaves repulsed three Hessian attacks. This was accomplished with some of the most fierce hand-to-hand combat of the entire war as the American troops, many of them armed only with knives, repulsed the Hessian bayonet charges.

As darkness approached, the fighting gradually petered out and the American army, tired from almost 36 hours without rest or food, retired to their camp as the cannonade continued throughout the night. It had been a glorious day for the American forces. On the following day, August 30, it became obvious that the French were not returning to aid in the battle.

When word reached General Sullivan warning him that the British fleet under Lord Howe, with 5,000 troops under General Henry Clinton, had been sighted off Block Island, the Americans felt there was no alternative but to retreat to Tiverton. Within a short time, as the militia units returned to Pawtuxet and Warwick from their heroic efforts in the Battle of Rhode Island, their feeling of accomplishment was great. They agreed with Lafayette's comment that "this was the best fought action of the war," but the fact remained that it was not a great and total victory. Despite the action on Aquidneck Island, the fear of an imminent British attack on Providence and Warwick persisted, and the forts at Warwick Neck and Fort Hill or Long Neck in Pawtuxet continued to be well manned.

In Warwick, the economic crisis worsened in 1778. Self-serving speculators, styled in the eighteenth century as "engrossers and forestallers," were buying all necessary articles, especially food and clothing, for private gain. Over 2,000 persons had been driven from Aquidneck Island as a result of the British action there. They were "homeless and penniless," dependent upon what little public and private charity was available. Warwick, already suffering, found little hope in caring for those who made their way to the town.

To make matters worse, on December 12, the area was devastated by a snowstorm. Historian S.G. Arnold reported, "The depth of the snow, and the intensity of the cold, was unparalleled in this vicinity. . . . Sentinels were frozen at their posts, or stifled by the whirling snow, and so many Hessians perished from cold and exposure on that dreadful night in Newport, that this gale was long known as 'the Hessian storm.' " Fortunately, by January 1779, other states came to the rescue of the Rhode Islanders suffering from the storm.

Finally, on October 11, 1779, 52 transports arrived at Newport and began to evacuate the 7,000-man British army. Sir Henry Clinton, the commander-in-chief of the British forces, feared an attack on New York and decided to abandon Rhode Island. The small state, while still suffering from many of the effects of the war, was at last free of the enemy within her borders.

The remainder of the year 1779 held both high hopes and bitter disappointments for Warwick and other Rhode Island towns. The joy of seeing the British finally evacuate Newport on October 25, 1779, was counterbalanced by the distressed condition of the economy and the adverse weather conditions, as severe cold once again struck Rhode Island. Prices soared, and in addition, the value of the currency plummeted despite all efforts of the state and the Continental Congress.

Major Samuel Ward Jr., a close friend and confidant of General Nathanael Greene, commanded the Black Regiment at the Battle of Rhode Island in 1778.

On May 19, 1780, a strange phenomenon of nature occurred that many Warwick residents felt was a bad omen, a warning of even greater reverses for the American forces in the Revolutionary War. According to S.G. Arnold's account, this "phenomenon, known as the 'dark day,' . . . occasioned much comment among the intelligent, and greatly alarmed the ignorant. . . . For several days the air had been filled with a dry smoky vapor, so that the sun could be looked upon with the naked eye, and the moon appeared as in total eclipse." Ships remained in the harbor at Pawtuxet and Apponaug while alarm and apprehension spread as the conditions worsened. Arnold's account continues, "On the morning of the nineteenth, this darkness increased. . . . so that candles were required at noonday, and all business was suspended." For many years, all uncommon weather conditions were compared to this day.

In 1780, a series of events occurred which affected a number of Warwick families. A definite ray of hope for American success began to shine through as the French fleet came into Narragansett Bay on July 10, 1780. On the national scene, the incompetent General Horatio Gates was replaced by Warwick's General Nathanael Greene. Greene assumed total command of the American forces in the South. This turned out to be the move that brought victory to the American cause. Historians agree that Nathanael Greene, next only to Washington, was the greatest American general in the Revolutionary War. Washington referred to him as his "good right arm." His action in the South harassed and weakened the British forces so that England, with all its power, began to feel that the war was not worth continuing. Greene's actions took so great a toll on the British General Cornwallis's forces that the British withdrew to Yorktown, Virginia. This proved to be a fatal error for the British forces in America.

The good news of a turnabout in the war in the Southern states reached Warwick and brought much happiness to the Greene family. Unfortunately, it was during this period that the Greenes were saddened by the news of the brutal killing of one of their family members, Colonel Christopher Greene. About 40 men of the Rhode Island regiment were killed, along with Greene, at an ambush on the Croton River in New York.

On October 18, 1781, Lord Cornwallis, British commander at Yorktown, Virginia, surrendered his entire 8,000-man army to the American and French troops. While it is true that the Battle of Yorktown was definitely a deciding factor in ending the Revolutionary War, it did not mark the end of the suffering on the part of Warwick and Rhode Island, as the war lingered on until April 1783.

It was soon obvious that the state's soldiers had returned home not only with their health impaired, but with empty pockets as well. The Continental, or paper, money issued by Congress was considered totally unsatisfactory. Soon the phrase, "Not worth a Continental," began to be used to show worthlessness and contempt.

Many of Warwick's soldiers, like Rhode Island's greatest Revolutionary War general, Nathanael Greene, returned home in 1783, and found the attitude of cooperation with the rest of the Union much changed. Problems quickly darkened the bright days and most of these were of an economic nature. While some Rhode Islanders prospered, notably Nicholas and John Brown, Nathanael Greene and many of his relatives did not. Nicholas Brown and his brothers were able to purchase the Potowomut estate of Richard Greene, a Tory. After the death of Nicholas, the brothers gave the estate to Nicholas's

Thomas Greene of Potowomut built this house in 1686. His grandson, the flamboyant "King" Richard Greene, was one of Warwick's most famous Tories. This structure is now part of the Rocky Hill School.

daughter, Hope Brown Ives, as a wedding present. John Brown had prospered to the degree that he built a magnificent mansion in Providence, and acquired John Greene's Occupastuxet estate in Warwick in October 1782. This property had been in the Greene family for over 140 years.

Because of the difficulties arising from war debts, Rhode Island soon found herself at odds with her sister states over raising revenue to support the federal government, which was in serious financial difficulty. Much of the problem stemmed from the inability of Congress to levy and collect taxes. To alleviate this condition, Congress asked for the power "to lay a duty of five per cent . . . on all goods, with certain exceptions, imported after May 1, 1781."

Eventually 12 states agreed, but Rhode Island refused, causing a crisis so severe that it eventually forced the abandonment of the Articles of Confederation as a form of government and brought about the necessity for drafting a new constitution. The arguments and discord in Rhode Island raged on from 1782 to 1790, with eventual disruption along political lines within the state which nearly caused a rebellion. During this period, Warwick, with both agrarian and mercantile interests, was divided.

During 1784 and 1785, the mercantile class in Rhode Island seemed to be in control, which greatly pleased the merchants in Pawtuxet and Apponaug. The popularity of the measures passed by the mercantile interests was very short-lived, both in Warwick and the state as a whole, as a new group emerged politically which controlled the state for the next four years. This was the "Country Party." It was dominated by the agrarian interests in the state and favored paper money laws. The party swept into power in 1785, and John Collins became governor, ousting the once popular William Greene of Warwick. It was not until May 1790 that Rhode Island eventually joined her sister states in ratification.

The ratification brought an increased prosperity to Warwick, especially to her seacoast villages. Much of this was due to the fact that shortly after Rhode Island became the 13th state to accept the Constitution as the law of the land, Congress passed an act, June 14, 1790, establishing customhouses in Providence and Newport. Two ports, Pawtuxet and Bristol, for the districts of Providence and Newport, respectively, were named as "ports of entry" or "Ports of Delivery."

There was a flourishing shipyard located just below the mouth of Pawtuxet Cove on the Warwick side where, according to local historians, the firm of Brown & Francis had their ship *Sally*. This 61-ton schooner, over 58 feet long, was built by the very famous Providence merchant John Brown and his son-in-law, John Francis. According to Pawtuxet historian Horace Belcher, the shipyard during the nineteenth century was owned by Benjamin N. Smith, who built the last ship launched at Pawtuxet under his own ownership and ran her in the West Indies trade. Belcher also points out that to provide the large quantity of rope used in the sailing industry, there was a ropewalk at "the

It is believed that George Washington, during his visit to Providence in 1790, rode in this chariot, built in 1782 for John Brown, one of the colony's most important figures. (Courtesy Henry A.L. Brown Collection.)

The black slaves and freemen who fought so valiantly in the Battle of Rhode Island are remembered for their contribution with this monument in Portsmouth.

Post Road end of present South Atlantic Avenue, in the rear of the Carr house, . . . and extending past North Fair St."

In addition to the ratification of the Constitution and the increased trade that resulted, there were two very significant measures passed in the late eighteenth century that affected some of Warwick's citizens. One of these acts, passed in 1783, gave Roman Catholics full rights of citizenship.

The second statute, calling for the gradual emancipation of slaves, passed in 1784, had its roots in the colonial period. As early as 1652, Warwick's founder, Samuel Gorton, then president of the colony, called for a general assembly, which ordered that "no slave, black or white, could be held in servitude for more than ten years." This was one of the first laws in the English colonies to provide for the emancipation of slaves. After a great deal of deliberation and discussion in the press, Rhode Island called for freedom for "all children born of slave mothers" after the first of March 1784. Warwick, with a large Quaker population, had very early shown her displeasure with slavery.

By the end of the eighteenth century, it was obvious that Warwick had played a significant role in the development of the early colonial period; that it played a key role in the movement for independence; provided many great heroes to the Revolutionary War; and participated in the emancipation of slaves and the freedom of religion.

While the town had only reluctantly agreed to ratification of the U.S. Constitution, it was able to reap the benefits of the increased trade and the stability that resulted from it. By the close of the century, Warwick was in the position of taking full advantage of the beginnings of the textile industry.

4. THE EARLY NINETEENTH CENTURY

At the beginning of the nineteenth century, Warwick's economic interests were primarily concerned with agriculture and the sea trade. Within a few decades, however, the town changed dramatically and, by the close of the century, was in reality two distinct entities economically and ethnically. The reason for the change was primarily the development of the textile industry in western Warwick.

The decade following the adoption of the Constitution by Rhode Island was exciting and promising for the seacoast towns. While Warwick was not directly involved in the East Indies trade, the ports of Pawtuxet and Apponaug benefited from the increased activity in Providence. The Jeffersonian Embargoes of 1805–07 and the War of 1812 dealt the maritime trade a severe blow. By that time, however, some of the profits of the China Trade and from the increased trading activity along the coast were already being diverted to the fledgling textile industry introduced to Rhode Island by Moses Brown and Samuel Slater.

As early as 1794, Job Greene, son of Revolutionary War hero Christopher Greene, helped establish Rhode Island's second textile mill in Centerville, which was then part of western Warwick. Very quickly, mills began to appear along the Pawtuxet River. Because of the availability of farmland, brought about by the decline in agriculture, mill owners not only purchased the rights to use the river and adjoining lands for their mills, they acquired tracts of land large enough to create nearly self-sufficient mill villages.

Mill owners seized the opportunity to establish paternalistic mill villages in which they controlled all aspects of the economic, social, and moral life of their workers. The social and intellectual thinking of the time believed that mill owners should control the villages as a father controls a family. In Warwick, entire families were recruited to work in the mills, and as the western sector of the town became industrialized, new villages came into being. As a result, the concentration of Warwick's population moved westward.

On October 3, 1794, shortly after Samuel Slater and Moses Brown demonstrated that textiles could be successfully produced in America, a company was organized to manufacture cotton by machinery. The site selected for this was on land in Centerville, once known as "Beaver Dam," which was owned by Job Greene, who operated a very successful gristmill and sawmill there.

By 1807, Almy and Brown had purchased additional land and all of Job Greene's rights to the spinning mill and had erected a second mill on the east side of the river. This new

The Bank Cafe was built by the Rhodes brothers in 1815 to take advantage of the increased sea trade and to serve as a bank for the new textile industry ventures of the time. In 1874, James Tinker established a fine restaurant here. (Courtesy Annie Totten Collection.)

mill was called the Warwick Manufacturing Company. The mill was originally painted green and became known as the "green mill."

Shortly after the mill was established at Centerville, the Rhodes family in Pawtuxet became interested in the new industry. Robert Rhodes and his sons had been very successful in the "coastal trade" and by the turn of the century expanded into other areas. Starting with a small gable-roofed mill, built south of the Pawtuxet Bridge, Christopher and William Rhodes made their successful entry into the textile industry. These brothers formed the C & W Rhodes Manufacturing Company and, in 1810, built a three-story mill on the northwest side of the bridge. This company was one of the first to manufacture broadcloth, and historian O.P. Fuller noted that this venture did "so well that the brothers extended their business to Natick."

By 1819, three companies were organized and a number of mills were built. In 1821, William Sprague of Cranston purchased two mills in Natick and brought what was to become one of the state's most significant textile families to Warwick. In 1852, the Spragues added to their interests in Natick by purchasing the Rhodes' holding there for $55,000.

The obvious advantages of the waterpower of the Pawtuxet River prompted the building of even more mills in Warwick's western section. In 1809, a partnership called the Lippitt Manufacturing Company invested $40,000 in the purchase of land and the erection of a mill close to the village of Phenix. The Lippitt Mill, near the intersection of present-day Main and Wakefield Streets, proved to be one of the few wooden mills to survive in Rhode Island.

While there were several houses and a small store in Lippitt early in the century, the village was regarded as part of the larger one at Phenix. The Roger Williams Manufacturing Company was built in that village at the northwestern corner of western Warwick. In 1810–1811, the Roger Williams Company built a dam across the river, several tenement houses, and a wooden mill.

Within the first two decades of the nineteenth century, several other villages appeared in western Warwick. In Crompton, the southernmost village in the western area of the town, eight men formed what was known as the Providence Manufacturing Company, and in 1807, built what is said to have been the first stone cotton mill in the state.

In 1813, on the south branch of the Pawtuxet River, not far from where it joins the north branch, Dr. Stephen Harris and Dr. Sylvester Knight decided to give up the medical profession and enter into cotton manufacturing with Harris's father-in-law, James Greene. In 1816, the mill failed and there was a change in ownership, which resulted in Dr. Stephen Harris taking control. Harris was very successful and by 1832 was operating one of the seven largest cotton mills in the state.

In addition to the excellent sites found along the Pawtuxet River in the western section of the town, Warwick also had fine water resources in Apponaug, which were used extensively in the early nineteenth century. During the eighteenth century,

This handsome structure, which stands on Centerville Road, was built by Caleb Greene in 1798. Caleb's son, George Sears Greene, one of the most distinguished generals in the Civil War, lived here. (Courtesy St. Barnabas Church Collection.)

Apponaug had been noted for its "fulling mill," which had been built by James Micarter in 1696. The Greene family of Apponaug acquired that mill and decided to convert it to textile manufacturing.

O.P. Fuller recorded that the fulling mill in Apponaug "was followed by a cotton mill, run by a company, of which Capt. Caleb Greene was the agent." Fuller described the mill as being "of three stories, shingled on all sides, and remained, until . . . the Print works went into operation. There was also a saw and gristmill in operation near by, for some years."

Caleb Greene Jr., who went from a sea captain to part owner and agent for a cotton mill, exemplified the trend in Rhode Island during the early part of the nineteenth century. In the period following the Revolution, Apponaug had become a very significant port, and Caleb Greene, whose ship was anchored in the Cove, was a prosperous mariner.

By 1803, war erupted in Europe between France, under Napoleon Bonaparte, and England. At first, these Napoleonic Wars seemed beneficial to Warwick and the American colonies, as the demand for goods kept prices and profits high. Soon, however, England attempted to stop trade with France by issuing Orders in Council, and Napoleon issued his Berlin and Milan decrees, which threatened to seize all ships trading with Britain.

In 1807, angered by these infringements upon the right of "freedom of the seas" and prompted by an attack upon an American frigate by a British vessel, which resulted in 24 Americans killed or wounded, President Thomas Jefferson asked Congress to enact an embargo prohibiting all foreign trade. This embargo proved disastrous for most New England merchants, who claimed their goods were rotting on the wharves. The embargo was repealed, but other acts that prohibited trade with France and England were passed that were almost as damaging.

In 1812, the United States and England were again at war and the Greenes of Apponaug turned toward the textile industry rather than the sea. The company, with Caleb Greene as its agent, prospered for a time. By the mid-nineteenth century, however, the Greene mills had suffered some financial reverses and the owners were persuaded to sell out their interests. This enabled a new group of entrepreneurs, led by Alfred Augustus Reed, who had made his fortune in the East India trade, to move into the area. One of his partners, Edward D. Boit, found Apponaug a most desirable site for the establishment of a print works.

The establishment of such a large enterprise as the Oriental Print Works meant a number of changes in Apponaug. The purchase by Reed and his partners included one large tenement house and one or two smaller ones. Hotels and boardinghouses, such as the Oriental Boarding House, owned by village butcher A.W. Hargrove, flourished in the early years of the Print Works. The mill attracted large numbers of workers, and unlike the early villagers, many of them were not of English or Scottish origin and were not Protestant but Irish and French Catholics. The increased activity saw Apponaug once again revitalized as an important center for business and trade.

Not long after the Greenes established their textile mill in Apponaug, a mill was erected in the area now called Pontiac. O.P. Fuller, in his history, noted, "No one of the villages on the Pawtuxet River and its tributaries has been designated by so many different names in the course of its history, as the one we have now come to." He traces the names back to

Early in the nineteenth century, this lighthouse was established to guide vessels through the narrow passage between Warwick Neck and Patience Island. It was erected at the tip of the Neck in 1826 and was dismantled in 1932, to be replaced by a more modern structure.

May 10, 1662, when it was called the "Great Weir," as many fish including salmon, shad, and herring migrated here and were caught with "weirs," or water traps. As the nineteenth century brought a great increase in the use of the river to power the cotton mills and dams made the natural migration of fish impossible, the weir was no longer in use. Fuller wryly commented, "the fish took offence, . . . and finally abandoned their old nurseries." The story goes on to say that later a bridge was built across the river, and the people, "like a drowning man, who is said to 'catch at a straw' . . . rechristened the place as 'the great bridge near the weir.' "

At one time, the bridge was called Captain Benjamin Greene's Bridge. Captain Benjamin Greene gave his land and homestead to his grandson, Benjamin Arnold. The bridge eventually was called Arnold's Bridge. It became especially well known when Henry Arnold, son of Benjamin, "kept a most noted public house," or tavern, there. The Arnolds erected a saw and gristmill along the river in 1810. Later, Dutee Arnold's son, Horatio, erected another mill and "carried on wool carding and cotton spinning . . . This building was also used for the manufacture of coarse woolen cloth."

Difficult times came to the textile industry in 1829, however, and the manufacturing operation at Arnold's Bridge failed. In 1830, John H. Clark purchased the land at auction and soon after bought the remaining mills still owned by the Arnolds.

Clark was very successful, and within a few years the village of Arnold's Bridge was more often called Clarksville. Clark, in 1832, built a stone factory for weaving and in 1834 constructed a large bleachery. Clark expanded both the weaving operation and the bleachery during the next decade and also operated a company store for his workers. O.P. Fuller credited Clark with bringing the name Pontiac to the village.

Clark, a very competent politician as well as a successful mill owner, decided to devote more time to politics. As a result, in 1850, he sold his interests in Clarksville. Zachariah Parker and Robert Knight purchased the mills for $40,000. Within a short time, Robert Knight contacted his brother, Benjamin Brayton Knight, and offered him a partnership. The Knights were able to buy Parker's share in the mill. This was the beginning of the

B.B.&R. Knight Company, which dominated the textile industry in Rhode Island for over 50 years.

As the mills waxed prosperous, there was a demand for better transportation to connect the mills of western Warwick with the seaports and major cities. As a result, the early 1800s ushered in the "turnpike era," which greatly facilitated bringing raw materials to and finished products from the mills along the Pawtuxet River. A turnpike (whether its surface was hard enough to turn the point of a pike or not) was a roadway controlled by a corporation that could legally charge tolls for profits and upkeep.

Christopher and William Rhodes of Pawtuxet were quick to realize the advantages of a road that would connect their textile mills to Providence and New London. Obadiah Brown, a shareholder in the Warwick Manufacturing Company in Centerville, joined the Rhodes brothers and several others in obtaining a charter in 1816 to establish a toll road, which was later called the New London Turnpike. By 1821, the road was completed and stagecoaches were operating on a regular schedule.

J. Earl Clauson, in *These Plantations*, pointed out that the New London Turnpike was 49 miles long. Some of the old timers who were interviewed by Clauson remembered the following:

> Toll charges at whole gates were 12 1/2 cents for a chaise, six cents for a man on horseback, six cents for a horse and wagon . . . A pair of horses paid ten cents. Cattle, sheep and hogs were taxed one cent per head. A "chariot" as private coaches were called, paid 30 cents, and the stage coach 20 cents.

While the New London Turnpike did provide a shorter route from Providence to New London, it was a financial failure.

As Apponaug grew in importance, this Town Hall and Town Clerk's Office was built in 1834–1835. The town was so rural that fences had to be put around trees to keep the cattle from destroying them. (Courtesy Henry A.L. Brown Collection.)

Apponaug residents enjoyed the service of Wilbur's store, located near the corner of Water Street and Post Road, in 1798 and the early nineteenth century. Later, in 1920, it became I.M. Gan's second store. (Courtesy Dorothy Mayor Collection.)

While Elijah Ormsbee of Rhode Island built a successful steam engine to power a boat on Narragansett Bay as early as 1796, it was not until 1837 that steam-powered locomotives brought trains through Rhode Island. In 1832, work began on the New York, Providence and Boston Railroad, known as the Stonington Railroad, and passengers were able to travel on it by 1837. From the very beginning of its existence, the Stonington Railroad made some significant changes. Its route closely followed the old colonial artery, the Post Road, and it rendered the New London Turnpike, which had become a major artery of trade, practically obsolete. Apponaug, because of its location on the Post Road, was given new life and its textile industry became even more prosperous.

In addition to the changes in Apponaug's textile industry, the railroad brought in a tide of immigration, which altered the old fabric of the village and brought in unimaginable changes. Prior to the coming of the railroad, Warwick had been almost totally inhabited by British-Protestant stock. In the 1830s, demand for labor to build the roads witnessed large numbers of Irish Catholics immigrating to Rhode Island. Old prejudices surfaced and a period of culture shock engulfed Apponaug. The Irish were encamped at Sweet Meadow Brook, adjacent to the railroad tracks in Apponaug. Local archeologist William S. Fowler found a number of artifacts in the upper 6 inches of soil in the excavated area that indicated the railroad gangs were there. They found white clay pipe fragments common in the early nineteenth century, a copper Roman Catholic religious medal dated 1830, an iron spoon, part of a china egg, scattered pieces of coal, some cut nails, a strap hinge, and a copper wire door hook. From this, Fowler concluded, "The workmen may have lived in huts; kept a few chickens; and worked small garden patches to help provide them with food." When the railroad was completed, many of the Irish remained in Warwick to work in the mills. Many of them went to the western section and by the late nineteenth century became a dominant force in areas such as Crompton, Centerville, Clyde, and Phenix.

During the first half of the century, a number of colorful politicians from Warwick played a key role in the state's politics. John Brown Francis, William Sprague, and William and Christopher Rhodes were among the most influential.

John Brown Francis dominated Warwick's political scene for a great many years. From the time he inherited the property from his mother, Abby (Brown) Francis, until his death, John Brown Francis made Spring Green in Warwick his home (1821–1864) and devoted his many talents to farming and to Warwick politics. He served Warwick on local, state, and national levels from 1821 to 1856. J.B. Francis was governor from 1833 to 1838. In that year, he was defeated in a bid for reelection by William Sprague, who, like Francis, had been a Democrat and Anti-Mason. In 1838, Sprague ran on the Whig party ticket. The change came about primarily as Sprague, a very wealthy manufacturer, believed the Whigs were much more in favor of "high protective tariffs" than the Democrats were. It was a very close election. Francis, who was defeated, polled 3,504 to Sprague's 3,984.

In the years following, Rhode Island was severely divided over the issue of political reform. In spite of the democratic trends started by Andrew Jackson, Rhode Island still adhered to its old voting procedures. In 1840, it was the only state that limited voting by property qualifications. Because the Charter of 1663 fixed representation, small towns controlled the General Assembly and the state. The movement for reform was led by Thomas Wilson Dorr, who bolted from the Whig party and became a Democrat.

In 1840, Dorr and his supporters formed the Rhode Island Suffrage Association and forced the legislature to call a Constitutional Convention. When the legislature ruled that only qualified property holders could elect delegates to the convention, the reformers demanded "popular sovereignty" and called for their own convention, allowing all adult, white male citizens the right to vote for delegates. As a result, two constitutions came into

During the nineteenth century, it became necessary to build better roads and turnpikes. Shares, such as this one sold to John Brown Francis, helped raise the necessary funds for the turnpikes. (Courtesy Henry A.L. Brown Collection.)

73

John Brown Francis's political career spanned a period of 35 years. He supported Governor Samuel King against Thomas Dorr in the 1840s. Francis served as Rhode Island governor and later, as a U.S. senator. (Courtesy Henry A.L. Brown Collection.)

existence: a "Landowners' Constitution" and a "People's Constitution." The "People's Constitution" was determined invalid by the Rhode Island Supreme Court.

The Dorrites refused to accept this and called for an election, choosing Thomas Dorr as governor. The landholders held an election shortly after and they selected Samuel Ward King as governor. King ordered the arrest of Dorr, who fled to Washington, D.C. to seek intervention from President John Tyler.

John Brown Francis gave his full support to King and the landholders. To counteract Dorr, Governor King sent Elisha R. Potter, John Brown Francis, and John Whipple, "three of our most distinguished citizens," to ask Tyler to intervene against Dorr. Francis and his colleagues were successful in keeping President Tyler from supporting Dorr and in assuring federal support to Governor King in the event of a rebellion.

Thomas Dorr, disillusioned by President Tyler's actions, returned to Rhode Island and set up a command post on Federal Hill. On May 18, 1842, about 230 Dorr supporters unsuccessfully attempted to storm the Cranston Street Armory and seize the weapons there to overthrow the Charter government by force. All of Dorr's attempts were unsuccessful, and in 1843, Dorr surrendered to the authorities and was imprisoned. Francis's support of the Law and Order Party during the Dorr Rebellion helped to minimize the divisions in Warwick that occurred during that period.

The defeat of Thomas Dorr and the quieting of the emotional upheavals of the "rebellion" did not mean an end to the reform movements, nor to the political power and influence of John Brown Francis. In 1843, an event occurred that, for a time, completely consumed the interest of the state and eventually thrust John Brown Francis into the U.S. Senate.

On December 31, 1843, Amasa Sprague, one of the owners of the very prosperous A & W Sprague Manufacturing Company, was brutally murdered. His brother, William Sprague, resigned from the U.S. Senate and returned to Rhode Island to take control of the family business and to attempt to find the person responsible for the murder. William Sprague also felt it necessary to assume responsibility for the training and welfare of Amasa's sons. To fill the vacancy in the U.S. Senate, the General Assembly selected John Brown Francis. Ironically, Francis was replacing the man who had defeated him for the gubernatorial seat in 1838.

Francis's senatorial tenure came at a time when the country was divided over the issue of the extension of slavery. This was brought to the fore when Texas, a slave-holding territory, asked to be admitted as a state. Once again, Rhode Island was the scene of bitter quarrels. This time the controversy was between those who favored annexation and an extension of the country's "Manifest Destiny" and those who advocated the abolition of slavery. John Brown Francis, whose grand-uncle, Moses Brown, had been one of the first to advocate the end of slavery in Rhode Island, voted against the annexation.

John Brown Francis declined to run again for the U.S. Senate, electing instead to serve as senator from Warwick in the General Assembly. Even in his declining years, when he suffered ill health, Governor Francis's council was much sought after and he was very influential in school and church reform and in political leadership.

One of the most influential of all politicians in the early nineteenth century was Christopher Rhodes, who lived in an imposing and beautiful home at 25 Post Road in the Pawtuxet section of Warwick. In addition to his early textile mills, a great deal of the success of Christopher Rhodes was due to his ability to recognize the need of adequate financing and cooperation among industrialists.

Christopher Rhodes's active political life spanned a time period of over half a century. From 1828 to 1831, he was the state representative for the town of Warwick and became well known for his strong stand on prison reform and on abolishing the whipping post and pillory as forms of punishment. As a result he was appointed to the building committee for the erection of a State Prison, which once stood at the northwest side of the Cove in Providence until it was razed in 1921.

A crisis arose in the 1830s on a social and fraternal aspect of village life when the Freemasonry movement was seriously jeopardized. The threat seriously affected the lives of a number of Pawtuxet's prominent citizens who were members of Harmony Lodge #9. At the height of the anti-Masonic hysteria, the Rhode Island General Assembly asked the Masons to discontinue and revoked the civil charters that had been granted to the lodges. In Pawtuxet, the Harmony Lodge went underground. By 1842, the Dorr Rebellion turned Rhode Island's attention from the Anti-Masonic movement and, within a year, the Masons were able to resume their meetings and the Masonic movement was again strong in Warwick.

Rhodes's political influence extended beyond his official capacities to his business acquaintances and his family members. The house at 25 Post Road was the scene of the marriage of Christopher's daughter Eliza to John R. Bartlett and of his daughter Sarah to Henry B. Anthony. Both sons-in-law became very powerful political entities and played key roles in the state's development.

During much of the nineteenth century, life was especially difficult for the minority groups in Warwick, as well as in the rest of the state. Prejudice, ignorance, and hatred unfortunately marked many of the relationships between the old Yankee Protestant stock and the Irish, French-Canadians, Swedes, Italians, and blacks. Ruthless politicians used the fear that the immigrants and the blacks, both of whom lived mostly in the cities, would take away rights and privileges of the white, agrarian majority.

Blacks in Rhode Island had to struggle for freedom and even when it was obtained, found they were still segregated, denied an education, and were relegated to the bottom of the economical scale. Warwick, as a strong Quaker settlement, expressed anti-slavery sentiments during the eighteenth century, and there were only 77 blacks recorded as living in the town in 1730. Some Warwick slaves were freed in order to join the celebrated "Black Regiment," which fought so well at the Battle of Rhode Island. Others, such as Boston Carpenter, were able to use their considerable skills to buy freedom for themselves and their wives and children. Carpenter had been a slave of Colonel Christopher Greene, one of Warwick's most renowned Revolutionary War heroes. According to historian Fuller, Boston Carpenter was "one of the wonders of those times. . . . [he was] a famous breaker of horses, an active mechanic and a quick, sharp man."

Many of Warwick's Quakers voluntarily freed their slaves and later supported the Gradual Emancipation Act of 1784. This act called for all children born of slave mothers to be free after March 1784. By 1807, nearly all blacks in Warwick were free. Freedom did not mean social equality, however, and even when blacks were able to buy land, deeds usually were clear to point out that the purchaser was "a man of color."

In 1823, the black community was dealt a severe blow when it was denied the right to vote. In 1824, and again in 1831, race riots broke out in Providence, and while rowdies set fire to some homes belonging to blacks, the police refused to interfere. In Warwick, in 1830, prejudice reared its ugly head at the State Fair in Pawtuxet. The *Providence Journal* reported, "We understand that John Proffitt, a colored man, died in Pawtuxet yesterday morning. His death was caused by blows inflicted on him by several persons the night previous. Several other inoffensive colored people were severely beaten and bruised at the same time and barely escaped with their lives."

When Thomas Dorr yielded to pressures by immigrant workers in 1840, and removed blacks from his call for Universal Manhood suffrage, many blacks who had earlier supported Dorr's pleas for reform now turned against him and volunteered to protect Providence against Dorr's followers. They were rewarded for their efforts in 1842 when the Law and Order Party adopted the Landholder's Constitution and added that black males over 21 had the same voting rights as white males.

While the blacks were encouraged to embrace Christianity, they found that equality did not extend to social or economic spheres. For the most part, they were segregated and held separate services. One example of this was the First Free Will Baptist Church, called the "Warwick Church," which had two congregations sharing the same buildings. During the Dorr Rebellion, one group, calling itself the Warwick and East Greenwich Church, consisted of blacks who favored the "Law and Order Party," which gave voting rights to black males. The other group, the First Free Will Baptist Church, favored the Dorrites. Despite the gains made and the good will of many in the town, the black community in Warwick continued to face a great deal of insidious prejudice.

Much of the mid-nineteenth century in Warwick was marked by a strong anti-Irish, anti-Catholic feeling. Henry B. Anthony launched his bitter campaign against the "foreign vagabonds" in 1838 and rode to power on a wave of nativism that engulfed the state. The Know-Nothing movement, blatantly anti-Irish in Rhode Island, put up a slate of candidates in 1855. They swept the entire state, including Warwick, and gained a majority of seats in both houses, electing William Hoppin as governor.

The major event that brought many Irish to Warwick was the coming of the Stonington Railroad to Apponaug. In the 1830s, demand for labor to build the roads meant large numbers of Irish Catholics, who took advantage of the lowering of fares in 1827. They were able to leave Ireland and find employment waiting for them in Rhode Island. Margie Bucheit, writing for the *Warwick Beacon* in January 1975, commented on the Irish in Apponaug with the following

> "Shack-town," an area along Sweetwater Brook was where, . . . laborers lived while building the tracks. . . . The workers scandalized Apponaug with their rowdiness, women smoking clay pipes and walking through town in their bare feet. . . . [the area was made up of] makeshift shacks, around which stood vegetable gardens and chicken coops. . . . the first train came through town, and the "shacktowners" moved on. With a sigh of relief, the men of Apponaug promptly burned their [the railroaders] shacks to the ground.

For much of the nineteenth century, the story of the Irish immigrant and that of the Catholic Church are closely intertwined. During the 1830s and 1840s, there were relatively few Catholics in the Pawtuxet Valley, and the nearest church to the Warwick area

The Stonington Railroad had a stop in Apponaug. It brought prosperity to the area and also provided employment for many Irish immigrants in the 1830s. During the nineteenth century, this signal tower was a recognizable landmark in Apponaug. (Courtesy Dorothy Mayor Collection.)

Dr. Charles Jewett was one of the leading Temperance lecturers of the early nineteenth century. Mill owners felt that, while they could indulge in alcoholic beverages, their mill hands could not.

was S.S. Peter and Paul's in Providence. As the Catholic population was still small, the diocese for the area at the time included Connecticut and all of Rhode Island. It was called the Hartford Diocese and Reverend William Tyler served as the bishop. By 1840, many of the Catholic families who walked the 10 miles to Providence every Sunday, often carrying their young children, supported Michael Carroll's request to the bishop asking for a priest for the Pawtuxet Valley. In 1834, Michael Carroll, his wife, and his brother, Edward, lived in the Clyde section of western Warwick and were responsible for getting permission from Bishop Tyler to have an itinerant preacher, Reverend James Fitton, celebrate Mass in Carroll's home in 1838.

During the early nineteenth century, the Reverend Fitton was asked to service a very large territory, which included Connecticut, part of southern Massachusetts, and Rhode Island. This was at a time when priests were still referred to as "Mister" and made their rounds on horseback. Because of the lack of communications, it was often difficult to place these early preachers on a controlled schedule. More often than not, they preached where and when they pleased and could not be depended upon to say Mass on a regular basis in the Clyde-Crompton area.

As the number of Irish Catholics began to flood the Valley after the potato famine, the need for a regular Mass and a church became evident. Unfortunately, anti-Irish prejudice made it practically impossible for Irish immigrants to purchase land from the predominately Anglo-Saxon Protestant landowners.

Fortunately for the newcomers, Paul Doran, a calico printer at the Crompton Print Works, and his wife, Mary, English Catholics, were able to acquire land in Crompton. An acre of land "on the hillside of the village" was given to Reverend James Fitton for the building of a church. Warwick had no Catholic church until 1844–45 in Crompton, which was then part of Warwick, and this church played an important role in the history of the town. This wooden structure, a relatively simple, one-story, shingle roofed building, was dedicated to Our Lady of Mt. Carmel and is known today as St. Mary's Roman Catholic Church, Crompton.

5. The Last Half of the Nineteenth Century

By mid-century, the population of Warwick had more than tripled, growing from 2,532 in 1800 to 7,740 in 1850. By the end of the century, Warwick's numbers had grown to 21,000. Much of the increase came from the influx of the first major immigrant group of the nineteenth century, the Irish. As the new immigrants were mostly Roman Catholic and Celtic, as opposed to the Anglo-Saxon, Protestant native population, prejudice soon reared its ugly head. Some mill owners, with very little compunction, used the prejudice as justification for keeping wages low, while unscrupulous politicians quickly saw the advantages gained by playing upon the nativists' fears of a growing foreign population.

The Civil War proved to be another turning point in the history of Warwick, as it brought unimaginable suffering for some and great wealth for others. Mill owners, while at first concerned with the lack of workers, found a new source of inexpensive labor in the French Canadian immigration. Unprecedented profits resulted from war contracts and great fortunes were made. The new "captains of industry" found Warwick ideal for establishing large estates along the coast and fancied themselves as the "landed gentry" of the New World.

In addition, Warwick became famous for its summer resorts. An especially significant one was Rocky Point, which had been started by Captain Winslow in 1847 as a place for steamboats to dock for Sunday school picnics. By 1884, Oakland Beach was also established in Warwick as a resort and playground area.

The Warwick Railroad, as well as steamboats, brought holiday crowds to these new amusement centers. By the end of the century, it became obvious that the needs, lifestyles, and problems of western Warwick and the area east of Apponaug were very different. For political, as well as for economic reasons, agitation for separation began during the last decades of the century.

By mid-century, it was obvious that the paternalistic mill villages were firmly entrenched and the mill owners were dominating the town. The Sprague family led the way as its textile empire grew and prospered. By 1821, the Sprague family became interested in the Pawtuxet River Valley and moved into the section. While Samuel Slater is usually regarded as the "father of the American textile industry," William Sprague, the sixth of that family to bear the name, is considered to be the man who developed it. Along with the purchase of mills in the area, Sprague obtained about 150 acres of land and the homestead of Thomas Holden in 1827. It is generally believed that before his death in

1836, he built the house at the Natick Farms that stands at 486 East Avenue. His mills and property went to his sons, Amasa and William, who formed the A & W Sprague Co., one of the leading manufacturing firms in the United States.

Amasa Sprague concentrated his attention to the business and lived at the beautiful family mansion in Cranston, while his brother William devoted much of his time to politics. William Sprague became the governor (1838–39) and a U.S. senator (1842–44). He made Warwick his country seat, added to the property, and developed a suitable "governor's residence" at the Natick Farm. William Sprague's venture into politics was cut short when his brother, Amasa, was murdered in 1843. This murder of one of the leading industrialists caused a great upheaval in the state. William Sprague retired from politics to devote all his time and energy to the family business, determined to find and punish his brother's murderers.

William resumed control of the family business, and under his very capable supervision, the company expanded. Upon his death in 1856, his son Byron and his nephews William and Amasa inherited a very prosperous financial empire. Byron was more interested in other developments, which included Rocky Point, and sold his interests to his cousins.

Under young William and Amasa Sprague, the A & W Sprague Mfg. Co. reached unprecedented heights. At the close of the Civil War, the Spragues' wealth was estimated at $19 million, and they employed over 12,000 workers. The Sprague mills and villages in Natick and Arctic, in western Warwick, were the prototype for many of the others in the valley. The Sprague mill system was definitely patriarchal by this time, and company officials wielded a great deal of power. While there was some dissension among the English, Scotch, and Irish workers, the French-Canadians accepted the concept of living in company houses and trading in the company store as a natural aspect of employment. William Sprague, sensing this, sent agents to Canada to recruit the workers he needed and, as a result, thousands of French-Canadians came to Natick and Arctic.

In some instances, they signed contracts to work for low wages for three years and to live in company houses. Most often they agreed to accept "script" rather than money. This was at the company's discretion if it felt it necessary to use cash for supplies rather than for the workers' salaries. The "script" could only be cashed at the company store.

The Sprague wealth and fame was so great that most Rhode Islanders believed the family was indestructible. In 1863, when William Sprague married Kate Chase, daughter of one of the nation's most important politicians, Salmon Portland Chase, the news of the wedding took precedence over war reports in many of the country's newspapers.

In 1873, the large Sprague empire began to collapse. William Sprague, the firm's leader, had become governor and U.S. senator and, while he achieved great success in many areas, he accumulated many enemies, invested unwisely, and speculated rashly. Jealousy, business rivalry, poor business practices, politics, and chicanery combined to destroy the largest textile firm in Warwick and in the state.

The fear of the loss of jobs and revenue to Rhode Island was great, but even Senator Nelson Aldrich, with all his power, was unable to stop the Sprague rivals from their destructiveness. By 1875, trustee Zachariah Chafee sold most of the Sprague holdings. Amasa Sprague was able to keep his large estate at Cowesett and Post Roads and William

The end of the old era of transportation saw this horse-drawn buggy making its way down West Shore Road at the intersection of Long Street. The railroad station and the Randall Harrington house can be seen in the background. (Courtesy Dorothy Mayor Collection.)

Sprague remained in possession of Canonchet, his lavish mansion in Narragansett, but most of the great wealth was stripped from the family.

In western Warwick during the mid-nineteenth century, the Lapham family shared a dominant position with the Spragues. During the latter part of the century, the influence of the brothers, Benedict and Enos, extended far beyond their factories in Centerville and enabled them to dominate Warwick politics for many years.

Benedict Lapham, a former blacksmith, started with a small workforce of about 85 employees, many of whom were children. There was no age restriction at the time and the wages were very low. Twelve-year-old "mill boys" worked in these and other Warwick mills for as little as $1 per week. This was accepted as normal since adult workers didn't earn a great deal more.

Fortunately for the textile industry in Warwick's western section, the boom years that followed the Civil War coincided with a necessity for many French-Canadians to migrate in order to find work. So many were employed in the Lapham and nearby Sprague mills that the ethnic makeup of Warwick witnessed a significant change.

In addition to controlling the mill workers' wages and housing, the Laphams attempted to control the morals and politics of the villagers as well. Enos Lapham was one of the strongest advocates of the temperance movement in the state, and he made every effort to keep alcohol out of Centerville and Warwick.

Enos Lapham provided the political leadership of Warwick for many years. Enos Lapham was very successful in his bid for public office. Like many other mill owners, he often spent lavishly to win, once allegedly giving $10,000 to the local Republican Party for his campaign. He was president of the Warwick Town Council in 1882, was elected to the Rhode Island Senate in 1886, and in 1888, as the unanimous choice of the Republican Party, was elected lieutenant governor. Lapham dominated the Warwick Town Council in

Robert Knight, a man with keen business sense, turned the Pontiac Mill and Bleachery into the base for a huge textile empire.

the late nineteenth century and was instrumental in starting the Kent County Water Authority and in building Warwick's Town Hall.

In a relatively short time, the firm of B.B.&R. Knight was able to use its considerable business skill to forge an even greater textile company than that of the Spragues. In 1883, the Knights purchased the four Natick mills for $200,000 from the Union Company, which represented the creditors of the Spragues. In the following year, the Knights bought the Spragues' Arctic Mill, one of the finest in the state, for $175,000.

Along with the mills, the Knight brothers also purchased much of the land once owned by the Spragues. In 1875, the "mansion estate near the village of Natick" came into their possession. They converted the East Avenue homestead of Thomas Holden and "old" Governor Sprague into a model "gentleman's farm" and showplace. A portion of this estate is now the Knight Campus of the Community College of Rhode Island.

The man responsible for this conversion was Robert Knight. It was he who first involved the family in the textile industry. His was the classic American story of the poor boy who worked hard and became rich. When John Clark decided to enter politics in 1850, he sold his mills to Robert Knight and Zachariah Parker for $40,000. Within a short time, Robert Knight contacted his brother, Benjamin Brayton Knight, and offered him a partnership.

Their success was phenomenal as they purchased many of the Sprague mills and consolidated and expanded. Benjamin Brayton Knight attended to the firm's finances while Robert Knight took care of the actual manufacturing of cloth. His skills in this area contributed a great deal to the textile industry in terms of remodeling and modernizing. He placed the four Natick mills under one roof and converted the mills into the largest and most modern cotton factory in the world during the late nineteenth century.

Robert Knight's sons and grandson inherited his interests. His son Webster Knight (1854–1933) learned the textile industry and gradually assumed control of B.B.&R.

Knight Co. In 1881, Webster Knight married Sarah W. Lippitt, also of a leading manufacturing family in the Pawtuxet Valley, and made his home in Warwick.

The prosperity of the Oriental Print Works, owned by the Reed family, declined in 1873. This was the year of a very serious "panic," or depression, which had a devastating effect on Rhode Island. In addition to this, the man behind the success of the print works in Apponaug, Alfred A. Reed, died in 1879, and by 1883, the company had ceased to operate.

Fortunately for Apponaug, the company was able to continue in operation after 1896. At that time it was known as the Apponaug Print Works. Due to technical problems, this company was dissolved and a new company, called the Apponaug Bleaching, Dyeing, and Print Works Co., was established and concentrated on the printing of staple cotton fabrics.

The American Civil War (1861–1865) marked a very definite turning point in Warwick's history. Many young men from the town's oldest families once again went to war. Fuller's history of the town lists at least 15 Arnolds, 6 Rhodes, 15 Greenes, and 8 Gortons in the ranks. They were joined by Braytons, Rays, Bennetts, and Browns. In addition, new names in the area were added from the ranks of the Irish who had come to build the railroad in the 1840s and who worked in the mills. Now names such as Carroll, Gallagher, Finnegan, Duffy, and O'Neill appeared with frequency in all regiments from Warwick.

The Civil War has often been called "the last of the old wars and the first of the new" because of advances in technology and military strategy. The same words can be used to describe the economic and social life in Warwick as tremendous changes resulted from the conflict. Warwick responded to all eight calls for volunteers and, as the war progressed, the list of dead and wounded began to grow. The death toll in this war was staggering. Over 1,300 Rhode Island troop members died in the struggle. The state contributed 28,000 men to the Union cause and 2,130 of these came from Kent County. Among the most famous Warwick heroes were Elisha Hunt Rhodes, George Sears Greene, Governor William Sprague, Samuel Dana Greene, and Charles R. Brayton.

Rhode Island, the last state to join the Union, was the first to offer to defend it as Governor William Sprague led the First Rhode Island Regiment to Washington, D.C. He was also present at the disastrous First Battle of Bull Run. During this fight, in which the First and Second Rhode Island Regiments took part, Governor Sprague narrowly missed death a number of times. In the panic that followed the Union Army's attempt to make an orderly retreat, 167 Rhode Island troops died. After this battle, the First Rhode Island Regiment disbanded and Sprague returned to Rhode Island.

The Second Rhode Island Regiment remained and went on to take part in nearly every significant action of the war in the eastern theater. One of the soldiers of the Second Rhode Island who captured the very essence of the war was Elisha Hunt Rhodes. He enlisted as a private at age 19 in 1861, and rose to the rank of colonel by the end of the war. Rhodes's story is eloquently re-told in *All for the Union*, edited by his kinsman Robert Hunt Rhodes.

Rhodes made it very clear from the very first that he was doing it "all for the Union." His letters bring forth an insight into the struggle that is unequaled. From these letters, Rhodes gives a thorough guide through the war, from the troops leaving from Providence, to the Potomac, to the Rappahannock (which he said, "resembles the Pawtuxet very much"), and on to the final victory at Appomattox. Rhodes participated in the first battle of Bull Run, where the nation learned of the horrible reality of war. He and the 2nd Rhode Island, along with the 4th, 7th, and 12th Rhode Island Regiments, were present at the tragic disaster at Fredericksburg on December 13, 1862. At this battle, the 12th Rhode Island was in the "hottest part of the fight" and lost 109 men killed or wounded; 16 of these casualties were from Warwick. Rhodes was also a participant in the Wilderness Campaign and in the siege of Petersburg.

While the battles were raging in the South, Warwick was the site of two camps. One, in Apponaug, was used to train recruits in the use of high-powered cannon. The other, Camp Ames in the Spring Green section, was the camp for the Third Rhode Island Volunteers, later called the Third Rhode Island Heavy Artillery. They left for the battlefield on September 7, 1861, where they were engaged in a number of conflicts. This group was led by Colonel Charles R. Brayton of Apponaug. He greatly distinguished himself in the Civil War and became a popular local hero. He was promoted to brigadier general and, as a reward for his wartime record, was made the U.S. pension officer after the war. This appointment was made available to him by U.S. Senator Henry B. Anthony. Brayton used this position to rally war veterans to Senator Anthony's party and together, Brayton and Anthony controlled Rhode Island politics for years.

Warwick's pride in the war was stimulated by the heroic actions of members of the Greene family. This family, which produced a number of great heroes in the Revolutionary War, contributed to the Civil War as well. The most famous family member was George Sears Greene, who was 60 years old when the war began. Greene, a West Point

General George Sears Greene, the hero of Culp's Hill at Gettysburg, was born in Apponaug in 1801. The Greene Memorial House on Centerville Road has been named in his honor. (Courtesy Henry A.L. Brown Collection.)

graduate who had served in the army from 1823 to 1836, recognized the need for trained officers and enlisted as a colonel. By the spring of 1862, his talents earned him the rank of brigadier general. Greene was made famous at Gettysburg when he led a heroic defense of Culp's Hill, which saved the Union army from disaster.

In the years following Gettysburg, Greene played an important role at the Battle of Wauhatchie, at Lookout Mountain, near Chattanooga. Again shunning the safety of a behind-the-lines position, he was severely wounded when a rifle ball passed through his face and damaged his upper jaw. Greene recuperated quickly and, undaunted, returned to fight beside his men, again placing himself in danger on a number of occasions. While George Sears Greene was distinguishing himself as a fighting general, his sons were also fighting in the war. One, Samuel Dana Greene, was the executive officer on board the USS *Monitor* and took part in the classic battle with the CSS *Virginia* (*Merrimac*) in 1862. Another son, Brevet Major Charles T. Greene was at the Battle of Ringold, Georgia, where he lost his right leg by a cannon shot. Warwick was well represented by the Greene family.

After the final surrender at Appomattox on April 9, 1865, ended the war, the conquering heroes returned to a Warwick that was visibly altered by the increased demand for textiles. Warwick was entering a new era. By the time the Civil War concluded, the Republican Party was firmly entrenched in Rhode Island and many of its leaders either came from Warwick or had direct connections with the town. During the early part of the century, John Brown Francis, John Waterman, Christopher Rhodes, and William Sprague were most influential, but in the period following the Civil War, the undisputed leaders were Henry B. Anthony, Charles Brayton, and Nelson W. Aldrich, and to a lesser extent, John R. Bartlett.

John Russell Bartlett was the son-in-law of Christopher Rhodes, one of the influential business and political figures of the early nineteenth century. Bartlett had earned a reputation as a leading writer and politician by the mid-nineteenth century. He was the Rhode Island secretary of state from 1855 to 1872. Among his most noteworthy accomplishments was that he helped create the boundaries for the state of Arizona, and was primarily responsible for the establishment of the Providence Athenaeum.

During the Civil War, Bartlett was acting governor from 1861 to 1862, while Governor Sprague took leave to command the Rhode Island troops encamped in Washington and in the First Battle of Bull Run. While secretary of state, Bartlett became deeply interested in the history of Rhode Island. For ten years Bartlett occupied himself in arranging and editing the state records. The result of this work is the 10-volume reference classic.

Another daughter of Christopher Rhodes, Sarah Aborn Rhodes, was also married in her father's house on Post Road. She married Henry Bowen Anthony on October 16, 1838. Like Christopher Rhodes's other son-in-law, Anthony had a brilliant career in literature and politics. After being a frequent contributor to and editor of the *Providence Journal*, Anthony became a joint owner of the paper in 1840. Henry B. Anthony was elected governor on the Whig ticket in 1849 and again in 1850. In 1859, he was selected as a U.S. senator and remained in that capacity until his death in 1884. Anthony was skilled at using the shortcomings of the Rhode Island Constitution to control the state. With the help of Charles Brayton, Anthony was, for many years, the "political boss" of Rhode Island.

Charles R. Brayton of Warwick was the acknowledged "boss" of Rhode Island politics. He controlled the Republican Party and the general assembly from 1865 to 1910. (Courtesy Henry A.L. Brown Collection.)

During the late nineteenth century, the man who perfected the Republican Party organization and managed it in the interests of Senator Anthony was Brigadier General Charles R. Brayton, a native of Warwick. Brayton was a member of a family which had lived in Rhode Island since 1643 and most often played key roles in politics and business. Brayton's grandfather was the Honorable Charles Brayton, a justice of the Supreme Court from 1814 to 1817 and 1827 to 1830. Brayton's father, William Daniel Brayton, was a member of Congress from 1859 to 1861, and his uncle, George Arnold Brayton, was chief justice of the Rhode Island Supreme Court in 1868. Brayton's father was in the lumber business in Apponaug and East Greenwich and served as town clerk of Warwick.

General Brayton entered Brown University in 1859, and at the end of his sophomore year, he left to volunteer in the Civil War. He recruited a company of the Third Regiment of Rhode Island Volunteers (Heavy Artillery) and offered it to Governor Sprague. He was appointed a lieutenant of the Third Regiment on October 9, 1863. Brayton was known as an excellent disciplinarian during his military career, and, although he was severe, he was popular with the men because of his gruff, easy manner. He distinguished himself on a number of occasions and, at the close of the war, Brayton, at age 25, was made brigadier general of volunteers.

Brayton built his political organization primarily on the votes of the rural and small-town Yankees who feared the incursion of the foreign populations in the cities. Brayton was director of several corporations and the careful guardian of the interests of the state's economic elite. He was the representative of both business interests and rural Yankees and elevated many small-town men to positions of leadership in the state. The power of the Anthony-Brayton machine came from what Brayton referred to as "old codgers" from country towns. Thanks to Brayton, they held all "key posts." Brayton made sure that no committee chairmen were all from the country and not from the cities. Through these methods, Brayton became the all-powerful "boss" of the Republican Party, and a nod from the general was enough to kill a bill.

When Anthony died in 1884, Nelson W. Aldrich took his place in Rhode Island political leadership and Brayton worked for him. Tradition states that when Brayton had become angry at one of the party regulars who wanted to run for Congress, the "Boss," looking for a new candidate, spotted Aldrich and threw his support to him.

In 1877, Brayton had feared that Aldrich might join forces with Henry Lippitt, the only possible threat to Senator Anthony's total control, and offered young Aldrich the governorship to win him over. Aldrich realized that being governor of Rhode Island at the time was at most an empty honor and turned the offer down. Brayton then offered him the chance to run for Congress in 1878. With the help of Senator Anthony and "Boss" Brayton, Aldrich was elected. In 1881, when Senator Ambrose Burnside died, Brayton and Anthony chose Aldrich as his successor. In 1881, U.S. senators were selected by the state legislatures rather than by popular election and, as Anthony and Brayton controlled the state legislature, Aldrich's election was assured.

Aldrich received the opportunity to begin a career that over the next 30 years would earn him titles such as "General Manager of the U.S.," "Boss of the Senate," "Commander-in-chief of the forces of protective tariffs," and "the most powerful man in U.S. politics." When he entered the Senate in 1881, it was estimated that his financial assets totaled about $50,000. When he left the Senate in 1912, his worth was calculated as upwards to $30 million and his estate was completed.

One of Warwick's most beloved politicians was Town Clerk James T. Lockwood, shown here in front of his office in Apponaug.

In the early 1890s, Senator Aldrich found Warwick Neck, with its quiet beauty, an ideal place to spend his summers. In 1896, he decided to make this his permanent summer home and purchased the Governor Hoppin farm and about 15 acres. Almost from the start, the senator envisioned a magnificent complex that would grow and develop over the years. Aldrich eventually purchased seven farms in the area to make this possible. He began this vast enterprise when he was 56 years old, and it was not completed until he was in his seventies.

During the nineteenth century, Warwick's 30-mile-long coastline gave birth to a number of resorts and amusement parks that made Warwick the playground of Rhode Island and the home of the clam dinner. Among these were Rocky Point, Horn Spring, Oakland Beach, Mark Rock, Gaspee Plateau, Buttonwoods, and Longmeadow. In addition were large landed estates purchased by the very wealthy in Warwick Neck, Potowomut, and along the Cowesett Shore.

Warwick's most famous summer attraction for over 145 years has been Rocky Point. Before 1847, Rocky Point, like most of Warwick Neck, was part of the farmlands that characterized the town in the eighteenth and early nineteenth centuries. In the 1840s, Captain William Winslow, part owner of the small steamboat *Argo*, saw Rocky Point as a desirable location to land his Sunday school excursion passengers. In 1847, Winslow received permission from Joseph Lyons to take his passengers ashore. Despite the tedious task of ferrying the passengers from the *Argo* to the rocky shore in small boats, the day was a great success. The following week, Winslow brought the Sunday school of Providence's First Congregational Church for an outing and started a tradition that continued for many years.

During the second half of the nineteenth century, Rocky Point grew to be the most popular amusement park in New England. (Courtesy Henry A.L. Brown Collection.)

Winslow, convinced of the potential of Rocky Point, purchased the 89-acre site from its owners, Mrs. Phebe Stafford Lyons and Mrs. Mary Stafford Holden for $2,400. Within four short years, "Winslow's Rocky Point" became the most popular shore resort on the bay. Winslow's first attractions included flying horses, the precursor of the carousel, swings, and a clamhouse.

Warwick historian Horace Belcher, who wrote extensively on Rocky Point in 1938, noted, " 'Mother Winslow' took charge of the clamhouse and the resort while her husband was bringing in excursionists on the Argo." Passengers, who paid 25¢ for the boat trip from Providence, were admitted to the park free of charge. By 1858, Winslow added bowling alleys, chariots, and a "Spanish fandango." The large wooden fandango was the forerunner of the Ferris wheel and was first seen in Rhode Island at Rocky Point.

The Winslows envisioned their park as a "clean resort," free of liquor and gambling, and hoped to attract church organizations for outings. They were very much dismayed when J.A. Littlefield established a resort called Horn Spring within walking distance of Rocky Point. Littlefield's resort featured a roulette wheel and other gambling devices and served intoxicating beverages. In order to keep Horn Spring patrons and other steamboats passengers landing at Littlefield's wharf from getting into Rocky Point free, the Winslows erected a high board fence and tarred it to discourage climbers.

Captain Winslow owned and operated Rocky Point from 1847 until 1865. During Winslow's period of ownership in 1860, David Stackhouse, noted Warwick historian, related that thousands were attracted to hear the country's foremost orator and leading presidential candidate, Stephen Arnold Douglas, speak at the park at the height of his popularity. In 1865, Winslow sold Rocky Point to Byron Sprague, who spent a small fortune in trying to make the park a playground for the very rich. He failed and four years later, sold the park to the American Steamboat Company, which later became the Continental Steamboat Company.

In the late nineteenth century, many mills and factories closed for a week or two in July and provided transportation to Rocky Point for their employees. For many, such as the English immigrants at Greystone in North Providence, this was as far as they ever ventured from the factory town in which they lived and worked, and for many mill workers, the day at Rocky Point was the most enjoyable day of the year.

The rich and the famous also came to Rocky Point. One of its most famous visitors was President Rutherford B. Hayes, who visited in 1877, the summer after becoming president in the disputed election of 1876. Hayes made history's first presidential telephone call when he called Dr. Alexander G. Bell from Rocky Point. Hayes later reported that he could understand words, but could not understand whole sentences.

In 1883, a spectacular fire demolished the Rocky Point Hotel. The fire started on March 16, before the season opened, when there were only a few employees at the hotel. Unfortunately, Warwick had no fire departments that could handle a large fire. There was a fire engine, called the Little Giant, on the premises, but it was inadequate for this task and a cry for help was sent to Providence. By the time help reached the park, the amusement center, the hotel, clam dinner hall, and boathouse were demolished.

The fire ended Rocky Point's dual identity as a resort for summer guests and day excursionists, as the hotel was never rebuilt. The park continued, however, to be popular for another hundred years. In 1888, Colonel Randall A. Harrington took control of Rocky Point and managed it through the first two decades of the twentieth century. Harrington excelled as a showman and entrepreneur and much of the prosperity of the park can be attributed to him.

The rise of Oakland Beach as a popular resort is usually dated from the 1870s. This is the time the Oakland Beach Hotel was built at the tip of the peninsula and when the Warwick Railroad ran its first passenger train from Providence to the beach. The history of the area, known as Horse Neck, can be traced to the very early Colonial period, but very little change occurred in the area until the 1830s, when people from the mill villages began to travel to the shore and when clambakes were given in nearby Nausauket and Buttonwoods. By 1870, plans were made for building a number of homes around Brush Neck Cove.

The Warwick Railroad, which ran its first train to Oakland Beach on July 4, 1874, had a great deal of confidence in the new development. It laid a double roadway across the peninsula along what is today called Suburban Parkway. It became obvious almost immediately, however, that the railroad was in difficult financial straits as they desperately tried to cut expenses. The line's schedules became so erratic that many came to believe that a trip on the railroad to Oakland Beach in the morning might not be followed by a return trip that night. In 1881, the Warwick Railroad passed into the hands of the New York, Providence and Boston line and rail travel to the beach improved considerably. The new owners extended the railroad across Oakland Beach to Buttonwoods. About a dozen well-built summer cottages were evident by the late 1880s, and the resort became very popular with tourists. It was at this time that the country's first "aquatic toboggan," the forerunner of the modern "flume," was built at the amusement park.

At the turn of the century, the railroad became the property of the Rhode Island Company and steam power was replaced with electricity. In a very short time, Oakland Beach became the favorite of Providence mill workers, who found transportation to the park inexpensive and easy.

In addition to the well-known resorts of Rocky Point and Oakland Beach, there were a number of hotels in Warwick that catered to a variety of tastes. Some, such as the Longmeadow Hotel and the Mark Rock Hotel, catered to transient visitors. The best known of these hotels was the one at Mark Rock, north of Conimicut Point, near present-day Rock Avenue. This house was located near a large, flat rock, which archeologists believed bore indications of Indian or perhaps Scandinavian hieroglyphics. Steamboats from Providence stopped here and, in a relatively short time, the Mark Rock Hotel became notorious as a drinking and gambling spot much like that at Horn Spring on Warwick Neck.

According to newspaper reports of the time, the patrons of the Conimicut resort were "thoroughly disreputable." The excursion boat which brought passengers to Mark Rock early Sunday morning would return later to gather their patrons after a full day of "carousing." It was common for a detachment of Providence police to meet the returning boat to arrest the "brawling, intoxicated revelers as they disembarked at the wharf."

With the coming of the Warwick railroad and the electric trolley, a great deal changed and improved along the Conimicut shore. A number of very well-built and maintained

It was in the late nineteenth and early twentieth centuries that crowds from Providence hoped to escape the oppressive heat of the city for the cooling breezes at Oakland Beach. (Courtesy Dorothy Mayor Collection.)

summer homes appeared and it became fashionable for Providence merchants, doctors, and lawyers to have a summer home in Conimicut. This well-established summer colony was able to demand laws restricting the gambling and drinking at the Mark Rock Hotel and to work towards closing it.

Members of the Cranston Street Baptist Church, appalled by resorts such as Mark Rock, and dissatisfied with the secular goals of most bayside developments, decided to establish a summer resort that would cater to the needs of religious Protestant families. They found that Fones Greene Hill, who had inherited much of the large Greene farm at Buttonwoods, was willing to sell a large portion of his farm. The Cranston Street group formed the Buttonwoods Beach Association to purchase that land.

This group was far from the first to see the advantages of Buttonwoods as a summer playground, as 30 years earlier, Buttonwoods was the scene of the first recorded clambake in Warwick. The clambake was a result of the presidential campaign of 1840. This campaign was noted as being one of the most flamboyant, "ballyhoo" type campaigns. The Whigs, a newly formed party at the time, which had William Henry Harrison as their presidential candidate, selected John Tyler as his running mate. With no real political platform, they relied on the old formula of "attract the voters with a free meal, get them in a mellow mood, pass out a few buttons, give a few speeches, and avoid the issues." It was felt that a good clambake would be a wonderful setting to sell "Tippecanoe and Tyler, Too."

Buttonwoods was selected as the site since it was not far from the main overland artery, Post Road, and it was easily accessible by steamship. In the 1840s, the site selected was on farmland and there was ample room for the large crowds, and the seaweed and shellfish were in abundance. The event proved to be such a success that many others followed and, in time, the Buttonwoods Hotel was built near the site of the 1840 clambake.

Buttonwoods Beach was ideally suited to those who wished to spend their summers away from the city and found the more popular amusement parks in Warwick too worldly for their taste.

The Reverend Moses Bixby and his congregation were very much impressed by the Methodist campground at Oak Bluffs, on Martha's Vineyard, and copied their example in Warwick. They formed the Buttonwoods Beach Association and laid down rules to develop the community according to their standards. The result was that Buttonwoods became a very picturesque community with a number of very beautiful, late Victorian cottages.

The resort quickly became popular and a horsecar line was built from Apponaug. By 1881, the Warwick Railroad was extended to Buttonwoods to provide direct access from Providence. By the turn of the century, there were 35 houses at the summer resort, and a number of prominent businessmen and their families found the area ideal. The Buttonwoods Beach Association has been very successful in keeping and maintaining the section in accordance with the high standards set in the 1870s.

In 1827 and 1828, a temperance society was formed in nearly every village in Warwick. One of the leaders of the Temperance movement who greatly influenced the town was James Burlingame, pastor of the Rice City Church. He was Rhode Island's first temperance agent and his sermons against alcohol often put him in physical danger, as at times stones were thrown at him and his sermons were interrupted. His efforts were rewarded, however, when he witnessed the state's first temperance meeting at the First Baptist Meeting House in Providence in 1827.

It was believed that Amasa Sprague was murdered in 1843 because of his strong opposition to liquor licenses. The death of Sprague and the controversy over the use of alcohol in the mill villages saw a statewide Prohibition Act passed in 1852.

As the Prohibition party grew in strength in Rhode Island, politicians such as Henry B. Anthony used the temperance men to his advantage. His enemies were accused of advocating the use of liquor and, one of his followers, the Reverend A.J. Woodbury, announced that "Candidates must be prevented from riding into power on a rum barrel and . . . should not be ruled by debauched Germans and ignorant Irishmen."

The Progressive element in the Republican Party in Warwick tried to use the prohibition issue to oust Webster "Boss" Knight and hamper the "machine" control of the town council. At a rally in Lakewood, the Citizen Party called Knight the "autocrat of the council table" and accused him of using his position to serve the B.B.&R. Knight Company rather than the citizens of Warwick. Foremost among the heated discussions at the Lakewood Town Hall was the controversy over the sale of liquor.

In 1886, a Constitutional amendment was passed in Rhode Island that prohibited the sale of liquor in the state. The Warwick Town Council, led by Webster Knight and heavily influenced by Charles "Boss" Brayton, sought to make the law ineffective. They appointed two special officers, Michael B. Lynch and Michael Kelley, for that purpose. These officers were instructed to ignore the violations of the law of 1886. It quickly became obvious that the law was unenforceable in Warwick. Many of the citizens who had voted Republican and were in favor of the temperance movement were angered at Webster Knight's casual treatment of the issue.

Bitter feelings grew as Charles R. Brayton, a noted tippler himself, had the state legislature enact a statute for the suppression of intemperance on May 27, 1886, and the very next morning appoint him to the newly created post of "Chief of State Police" to enforce the law. Brayton abused the office so terribly that, although elected for three years, he was actually forced to resign the position.

According to the *Pawtuxet Valley Gleaner*, the area's local newspaper, special officers would go to the most notorious areas of Warwick, raid one establishment there, where the owner was known to be against Brayton's machine, and then stand on a corner where they would be conspicuous. After a while, they would slowly walk down the street and investigate establishments under complaint. Needless to say, with all that warning, there were few, if any, arrests.

Voters believed that this was done with Knight's knowledge and consent. It led to his defeat in 1898 and to the victory of the Citizens Party coalition. The newly elected town council was able to enact some reforms and, for a very short period of time, even the illegal sale of beer at Rocky Point was curtailed. By the end of 1899, however, the General Assembly was forced to agree with Brayton that the law was unenforceable and prohibition was soon repealed.

While the Irish were the largest group of immigrants to make an impact on Warwick by mid-nineteenth century, they were not alone. During the late nineteenth century, large numbers of British and French-Canadian workers were found in all the town's villages, and by the end of the century, they were joined by immigrants from Sweden, Poland, the Ukraine, Italy, and Central Europe.

From the very beginnings of the textile industry, Warwick manufacturers turned to the British Isles for the skilled craftsmen they so desperately needed. If the new industry was to succeed, it would require the services of specially trained craftsmen. During the 1860s, large numbers migrated to Pontiac from the heavily industrialized areas of England. Many were from Lancashire and were accustomed to the paternalistic mill villages there. As they had in England, most British immigrants worked at the mill, lived in mill houses, read the mill newspaper, traded in the mill company store, and attended Episcopal church services arranged by the mill owners.

In 1875, Thomas Jefferson Hill named this steam-powered 20,000-spindle cotton mill in honor of his wife, Elizabeth Kenyon Hill.

Despite the gains made by the Constitutional amendments following the Civil War, the black population in Warwick continued to be harassed by prejudice and intolerance. Even in the field of religion, disputes continued. The bitterness within the church at Hillsgrove lasted well into mid-century. The Dorrite faction of the Free Will Baptist Church refused to let the blacks use the building, where they had previously conducted services.

Fortunately, a number of citizens, led by John Brown Francis, came to the aid of the displaced parishioners and helped them to build a church on the "Plains," as Hillsgrove was then called. This church, known as the "colored" church, was consumed by fire in 1873. By this time, the bitterness of the Dorr rebellion had passed and the First Free Will Baptist Church sold their building on Post Road to the black Warwick and East Greenwich Free Will Baptist Church.

Historian Fuller notes that in 1875, there were five Catholic parishes in what were then villages in Warwick. These were located in Crompton, Phenix, Centerville (Arctic), Apponaug, and Natick. In regards to the one in Natick, St. Joseph's, Fuller mentioned that "within the past three years, a church has been erected to accommodate the Catholic residents of that village, and the resident pastor, Rev. Mr. Reviere, preaches to two distinct congregations at different parts of the day—to one in English and to the other in the French language."

In 1844, when St. Mary's Church was built in Crompton, any hope for a Catholic church in Apponaug still seemed far in the future. By the Civil War, however, the increase in industry had resulted in even more Irish working in the Oriental Print Works in Apponaug. By that time, there were enough Catholics in the village of Apponaug that Reverend William Halligan came from East Greenwich twice a month to offer Mass at the old Town Hall. By 1873, the Catholics were numerous enough to call for the construction of a small 24-by-60–foot gable-roofed building on Greenwich Avenue. It served as a "church and mission parish," administered by priests from East Greenwich.

Unfortunately, 1873 was a year of a very serious economic panic and this seriously curtailed the textile industry at the time. Unstable working conditions meant no increase in the Irish and French Catholic immigration for awhile and no substantial church building was done in Apponaug until after the turn of the century.

As the number of both Irish and French Catholics grew in Hill's Grove, a mission church was started in that village in 1900. Missionaries of the Sacred Heart, which had taken charge of St. Joseph's Parish in Natick in 1899, sent priests to Hill's Grove weekly to celebrate Mass. The earliest priests celebrated Mass at the public school for a brief time, until May 1900, when the small Mission Church of St. Francis was built.

The need for laborers in the mills coincided with economic depressions in French Canada, and soon a steady stream of French-Canadians could be found coming into the Pawtuxet Valley. To the economically distressed French Canadians, the wages paid by Warwick mill owners, while low by Rhode Island standards, were acceptable. A grateful and often docile immigrant, used to near starvation in his native land, seemed able to thrive on "any kind of food, wearing the shabbiest clothes, and having the worst housing."

An outstanding group of immigrants that made a great impact on Warwick were those emigrating from Sweden who came to work in the mills at Crompton and Pontiac. Early records show that "The first Swede to move into the area was Andrew P. Magnuson from Hossna, Sweden. He came with his wife, daughter and two young people." Soon, many others left Vastergotland and Gottenburg to settle in Pontiac. From Pontiac, the Swedes moved into other parts of Warwick as new employment became available. So many Swedish immigrants settled in the section around East Greenwich Avenue that the area became known to many as "Swedie-ville." The Swedish population in Pontiac played a significant role in the development of the Lutheran church there and in the success of the Knight Mills in that village.

PONTIAC ROAD NEAR FOUR CORNERS, APPONAUG, R. I.

The major artery connecting the mills at Apponaug with those at Pontiac was this dirt road, known as Pontiac Road and later as today's Greenwich Avenue. (Courtesy Dorothy Mayor Collection.)

Near the very end of the century, Warwick, especially in the western villages, was home to a growing number of people from Poland, Canada, the Ukraine, Czechoslovakia, and Bohemia. They were soon joined by a tremendous wave of immigration that added the Italians to Warwick's growing number of foreign-born workers.

By the last quarter of the nineteenth century, it was evident that Warwick had become two very distinct entities. The western area, with its mills and ever-increasing number of non-English–speaking mill workers, contrasted sharply with the "Yankee," agrarian, coastal eastern section. All efforts to achieve a division of the town were successfully blocked by master politician Charles R. Brayton. Upon the death of his supporter and mentor, Senator Henry B. Anthony, Brayton found that he was the undisputed controller of the Republican Party in Rhode Island. Within a relatively short time, however, new *Providence Journal* owners and staff began to attack Brayton and "bossism." The paper charged that Kent County was especially corrupt and in 1888, tried to stop the election of Centerville mill owner Enos Lapham as lieutenant governor. They charged that Lapham openly bought votes for his election. The charge was that Brayton had collected so much money that the Republicans were willing to pay any voter $15 "to vote for his principles."

P.H. Quinn and other politicians in western Warwick tried making a strong case for a division of the industrial west from the agrarian east, but Brayton objected, knowing full well that a separation would mean the new town, with its mill workers and immigrants, would vote Democratic. Even Brayton could not stop progress, however, and as the century came to a close, Warwick was beginning to feel the impact of changes being made by new inventions and new standards of living. While it would be a long time before the average workers would reap the benefit, they were aware that a new world was possible.

In the 1890s, when this photograph was taken, Hoxsie was primarily noted for its agricultural products. Members of the John Olney Nelson Hoxsie family are shown here. (Courtesy Hazel Crandall Collection.)

During the late nineteenth and early twentieth centuries, the Apponaug Hotel played host to visiting businessmen who came to deal with the Apponaug Company, the leading textile firm in the Pawtuxet Valley.

By the 1890s, gaslights were common, antiseptics and sterile bandages were coming into their own, and even deodorants were gaining acceptance. Howe's sewing machines would soon revolutionize the dressmaking and shoemaking industries, and while textiles still ruled, other industries were coming to the Pawtuxet Valley.

In addition, Rocky Point was growing rapidly as an amusement center and it continually added new attractions, even making provisions for "base ball" (always spelled as two words in the nineteenth century), the new craze sweeping the country. These early games were anything but pitchers' duels, as many of the scores were in double-digit numbers. By the closing years of the nineteenth century, the "new game," introduced by the Knickerbocker Club in New York, had become popular in Warwick. Within a few years, there were over 200 teams playing amateur ball and many of them made their way to Rocky Point.

While most were enjoying the new pastime, the "sport," many claimed, was attracting an unsavory element to Warwick. Rowdies from Providence, residents charged, came through Lakewood to play at Baker's Station, 1 mile below the village. They believed that, after the game, these "rowdies" were drunk and harassed the neighborhood. The situation became so serious that new constables had to be added to the Warwick police force. In 1883, in Apponaug, a special ordinance was passed regarding base ball, as "several persons have been hit with balls, and a number of horses frightened while passing through the streets of this and other villages in Warwick." The town council stated, "The playing of base ball, practicing with base balls, the throwing of balls, stones or other missiles in the public streets and highways of said town, is hereby prohibited."

Of a much more serious nature was the problem of fire. As the century drew to a close, larger and better equipped fire companies were deemed a must. While community fire brigades had been in existence since colonial times, nearly every major mill in Warwick had a fire department of its own. Unfortunately, these were often small and poorly equipped.

The first ordinance creating a fire company in Warwick was recorded in 1817. At that time, according to records found by historian Henry A.L. Brown, the General Assembly was petitioned for permission to organize an "Opponaug Fire Company" to protect the village of Apponaug. The monies raised by taxation were to be used to purchase an "engine, apparatus, ladder, hooks, etc." By 1865 there were a number of volunteer fire companies formed that used hand-drawn pumpers. In 1872, a fire company was formed in Apponaug and was called the Vigilant Fire Company No. 1.

By the turn of the century, there were volunteer fire departments in a number of areas. The Lakewood Fire Brigade, later the Cataract Fire Company No. 2, was formed in 1891 and the Warwick Fire District was created in 1889 to help care for the western section of the town. In 1907, it also included Read Avenue in Coventry and the name was changed to the Warwick and Coventry Fire District.

As the century closed, there was an ever-increasing clamor for political reforms and for greater services for the town. The seeds planted in the nineteenth century eventually came to bear fruit in the twentieth.

In 1898, a large crowd gathered at the Apponaug Railroad Station to see Presidential candidate William Jennings Bryan, shown here with members of the Compston family. (Courtesy Dorothy Mayor Collection.)

6. WARWICK TO 1930

Warwick in the twentieth century evolved from a town of 21,000 residents, living in loosely connected mill villages and small farms, to the second largest city in Rhode Island, with a population of over 85,000. The transition was not an easy one. The town, after bitter political machinations, was divided in 1913, when the Town of West Warwick was created. Warwick lost 8.3 square miles of territory, one half of the population, and almost all of the town's industrial base. The only major mills that remained in the 36.26 square miles of Warwick were the Elizabeth Mill in Hillsgrove, the Apponaug Company, and the Pontiac Mill. These were, at the time, all thriving and valuable assets for the town.

The division emphasized Warwick's role as an agricultural community with the needs of poultry and dairy farmers once again occupying much of the town's business. The trolley line, which was established in 1910, made it much easier to commute to Providence and Cranston. This improved mode of transportation, followed by the increased use of the automobile, saw many transforming their summer residences into year-round homes. With the aid of better transportation, Warwick became the summer playground for the middle class of the state. Oakland Beach, Rocky Point, Mark Rock, Warwick Downs, Buttonwoods, Gaspee Point, Nausauket, and Longmeadow all benefited.

As World War I introduced Warwick and Rhode Island into a much larger world, new problems arose that showed the town at a disadvantage. Nineteenth-century fire-fighting methods proved inadequate and slowly, but surely, improvements were made, but only after a series of devastating and heart-breaking fires. Around that time, the great textile industry began to weaken and totter. Strikes, layoffs, and outside agitators plunged the area into an early depression.

Prohibition, long sought after by some elements, proved unenforceable. Warwick's small-town police force could do very little to stop the speakeasies that "grew like Topsy." The gangster element soon found the town ideal for their operations. Once again, smuggling became a common event as the understaffed police force proved to be inadequate for the task. Now, instead of the molasses and sugar that was smuggled in the eighteenth century, liquor was finding its way to Warwick's small coves and harbors.

In 1929, Warwick's Hillsgrove section was selected as the site for the state airport, creating the catalyst that would greatly alter the town's environment. The new facility opened on September 26, 1931, attracting a crowd of over 15,000. Warwick's population

Thomas Hill's Malleable Iron Works employed many immigrants during the early twentieth century. These workers were given a short break while this photograph was taken. (Courtesy Dave Matteson Collection.)

in 1930 had recovered from the loss due to the 1913 separation and, in 1931, Warwick became Rhode Island's seventh city. Its voters approved a charter for a mayor-council plan of city government. During the next decades, the new city struggled through the poverty of the Great Depression, the devastation of the Hurricane of 1938, and the trauma of World War II.

While the city was zoned for residential, farming, business, and industrial districts, the increased migration to Warwick and other problems created by the Depression and the hurricane often turned well-intentioned plans into haphazard growth, resulting in the destruction of some of Warwick's finest attractions. In the five-year period following World War II, Warwick's population soared from 28,000 to over 40,000. This created a demand for more housing, more adequate schools, police and fire departments, and other improvements.

During the early years of the twentieth century, Warwick became a major area of employment for immigrants from Central and Southern Europe, a summer playground for the middle-class workers, and a country retreat for the very wealthy. The B.B.&R. Knight Company was the chief employer in the Pawtuxet Valley, and they hired many Italian, Polish, and Ukranian immigrants to complement the workforce of Irish, French-Canadians, and Swedes.

The large influx of Italian immigrants to Rhode Island was amazing. In 1900, there were nearly 9,000 residents who were born in Italy and, by 1910, the number rose to 27,287. Most of those who took part in the great migration from 1898 to 1932 were from southern Italy and, while they were predominantly farmers, they came to work in the mills. Many of those who settled in the Pawtuxet Valley were hired by B.B.&R. Knight Company mills in Natick and Pontiac. They worked in the mills when the average weekly take-home pay for textile workers was $14. In most mills of the Pawtuxet Valley, the Italian immigrants averaged less, often getting only $10 per week. They lived in company housing where the rent was cheap, approximately $1.25 per week. Even low wages, measured by American standards, were high wages to Italians and to the many Polish and Ukrainian immigrants who came to Warwick around the turn of the century.

Many of the new immigrants took in boarders from their homeland. In time, so many took advantage of this type of arrangement that beds were usually cots, and "spaces" rather than "rooms" were rented by the newcomers. As space was at a premium, most "boarders" were relatives, or came recommended by relatives or friends. The usual charge for "room and board" was 25¢ per week. Women who prepared their own meals and who helped feed the other boarders frequently paid less.

The mill villages were, in effect, divided along ethnic lines physically. In Pontiac, for example, most of the Swedes lived in the vicinity of King, North, and Central Streets and owned their own homes. The area was known to many as "mortgage hill." The section of Pontiac below the tracks, on what was then Railroad Street and is now West Natick Road, was inhabited by Italian and French-Canadian workers, most of whom lived in company houses and paid rent to the B.B.&R. Knight Company. The divisions were obvious not only in the housing and the positions held in the mill, but in the choice of churches as well. Religious services in French, Italian, and Polish became more common as the large numbers of immigrants entered Warwick.

One significant impetus to the shore resort trade in the early part of the century was the development of the trolley system in Warwick. During the nineteenth century, public transportation was confined primarily to horse-drawn vehicles of the Union Railroad, which had been established by Amasa and William Sprague in 1865. When the Sprague

These well-groomed scholars attended the Buttonwoods School in 1904–1905. (Courtesy Dave Matteson Collection.)

101

textile empire collapsed in 1873, a group of stockholders headed by Jesse Metcalf, prominent Providence businessman and part owner of the *Providence Journal*, purchased the Sprague horsecar trolley enterprise. Metcalf led the way for a drive to electrify the horse-car railway and was successful by 1892, when the first electric trolley was operating in Providence. Realizing the potential for immense profits and the necessity for large outlays of money to accomplish electrification of the various steam locomotive lines in the state, a syndicate was formed to purchase the Union Railroad. This syndicate was headed by Senator Nelson W. Aldrich, Marsden J. Perry, and William C. Roelker.

A large portion of the funds raised by this group came from the American Sugar Refining Company, which had close economic ties with Senator Aldrich. The funds obtained were used to finance and electrify car service in the suburbs. The Warwick Railroad, which had been chartered in 1872, was sold to the Rhode Island Suburban Railway Company, and in 1902, the Union Railroad was reorganized to form the Rhode Island Company, which connected a large number of local companies. In 1906, J.P. Morgan, director of the New Haven Railroad, purchased the Rhode Island Company and Aldrich, Perry, and Roelker made an alleged $15 million profit. Under Morgan, the Rhode Island Company took control of the Rhode Island Suburban Railway, and the trolley became a common sight throughout Warwick and the Pawtuxet Valley.

The electric trolley captured the imagination and support of Rhode Islanders as the new system proved faster and quieter than the horse-drawn railroad and it was cheaper, cleaner, and more efficient than the steam locomotives. The vast networks of trolley lines were all powered by 600-volt DC current and were all standard gauge. The current was provided to the cars by an overhead wire, hence the name "trolley."

By the end of the first decade of the twentieth century, trolley lines ran from Providence through all of eastern Warwick. The route followed the old Warwick Railroad line to Buttonwoods and went on to Westcott, where there was a power sub-station to

Senator Nelson Aldrich's mansion, Indian Oaks, was completed in the early twentieth century. Aldrich, a connoisseur of fine art, tastefully decorated the interior with masterpieces. (Courtesy Reverend Edmund Fitzgerald Collection.)

This view was taken looking east from the four corners in 1919. Note the drugstore in the Gilbert Building and the trolley tracks. (Courtesy Bob Champagne Collection.)

complement the main power base on Manchester Street in Providence. At Westcott, the lines connected with the Providence-Riverpoint-Washington line and with the Hope-Crompton line at Riverpoint. In addition, the East Greenwich line, which extended to Wickford, was intersected at Apponaug. In Warwick, the trolleys were housed at the Rocky Point and Riverpoint car barns and at the Clyde car barn.

Historian Horace Belcher, writing about the old Warwick and Oakland Beach Railroad, reported that fares were low on the new trolley line. For passengers without baggage, the fare to Auburn was 5¢ and to Lakewood, Shawomet, Riverview, Bayside, and Old Warwick, it was 10¢. For the longer ride to Oakland Beach and Buttonwoods, the fare was 15¢.

Along with the trolley's growth and success, there were also serious problems. When a head-on collision of two trolley cars on June 10, 1900, occurred in Warwick, resulting in the death of 4 and the injury of 28 passengers, double tracks and automatic signals were introduced for safety. Working conditions on the trolley lines were very poor. Scott Molloy, in his research on streetcar employees, cited a number of cases where conductors worked under extremely poor conditions. Molloy noted, "Italian workmen were singled out for special discrimination . . . they worked almost exclusively on the low paying track gangs. . . . They had to bribe the foreman ten dollars to get the job and leave fifty cents thereafter in the boss' hat on payday."

There was often extreme overcrowding on the cars, very poor heating in the winter, and inadequate ventilation in the summer. Despite these shortcomings, the trolley provided an escape from the bonds that had tied mill workers earlier. With inexpensive and relatively fast transportation, workers no longer had to live in the vicinity of their employment and could travel farther to seek higher wages and better working conditions. In addition, the trolley provided the means for workers to leave their hot, crowded homes in the summer

This drawbridge went across Warwick Cove and brought passengers to Oakland Beach near the Pleasant View Hotel (later the Bayview Restaurant). (Courtesy Henry A.L. Brown Collection.)

for a day of pleasure at Warwick's shore resorts. This demand for transportation resulted in a 1/2 mile line built from Grant's Station, below Longmeadow, to Rocky Point, and another from Buttonwoods to Westcott. In the summers, "bloomers," or open cars, were in use and thoroughly enjoyed as a great adventure by large crowds who looked forward to a 20-minute ride on the trolley from Arctic to Oakland Beach via Tollgate Road and Apponaug.

When the trolley was at its peak, there was a natural alliance between the proprietors of the trolley lines and the owners of the amusement parks. The electric streetcar lines very often advertised the attractions of the parks and, on occasion, contributed their own personnel to help build and maintain the resorts. The parks, in return, encouraged people to come by trolley and often included trolley schedules. The powerful drawing cards of the concerts, clambakes, dances, and popular amusements increased the need for more trolley cars in the summer. Two of the resorts that prospered greatly by the trolley in the early twentieth century were Rocky Point and Oakland Beach.

In time, the automobile and bus brought about an end to the trolley car. By the 1930s, streetcar companies found the long lines to the suburbs were not economically feasible and the streetcars were operated only on an intra-city basis in Providence.

In 1911, R.A. Harrington purchased Rocky Point Amusement Park from the Providence, Fall River & Newport Steamship Company and ended wild speculation concerning the future of the park. Colonel Harrington announced that he would keep the site as a summer resort and would add amusements so that the Warwick park would rival that of Coney Island. Harrington leased the park in 1888, and by 1900, his flair for the business had already made him the most popular resort proprietor in New England. He advertised extensively and drew customers from as far away as Maine and Canada. The excitement of going to Rocky Point was so great that often excursions of hundreds arrived accompanied by their own bands. During the height of the season, trolley cars ran from Providence every five minutes, and boats came into the wharf on an hourly basis.

One of the most heralded events was the Rocky Point Clam Dinner. These dinners were so popular that over a hundred bushels of clams a day were consumed and, under Harrington, the shore dinner hall was enlarged to a seating capacity of 2,500. One of the most memorable clambakes was that held for the 40th reunion of the Army of the Potomac in 1904, when over 250 veterans and their guests came from all areas of the United States.

Advertising brochures in 1913 pointed out, "In short, Rocky Point is a park of eighty-nine acres bristling with attractions at every turn, so varied that everyone finds his favorite recreation as so tremendous in extent that with a throng of 75,000 people on the grounds, there is still room for many thousands more." In the early 1900s, the park had a large bandstand on the Midway, a "New Carousel" with four rows of jumping horses, and an $8,000 organ, "largest and finest in America, which produced the effect of a 60-piece band."

Under Harrington's leadership, Rocky Point always presented something new and exciting and catered to many different interests and tastes, from opera presentations to the latest vaudeville acts. For those whose love for baseball was great, Harrington arranged for the Providence Grays to play their Sunday home games at the park's baseball diamond. Here, on almost any Sunday, a thousand spectators would pack the bleachers and grandstand to watch the Grays create baseball history. The Rocky Point Ball Grounds were also available for field sports or contests of any kind, and this was a major attraction for ethnic groups and mill-sponsored teams.

Oakland Beach also prospered as a result of the trolley. When the Warwick Railroad passed into the hands of the New York, Providence and Boston line, the railroad tracks were extended across Oakland Beach to Buttonwoods. In 1900, the road became the property of the Rhode Island Company and steam power was replaced with electricity. Within a very short time, the trolley helped make Oakland Beach the favorite with Providence mill workers, as now transportation was inexpensive and rapid.

Oakland Beach had the country's first "aquatic toboggan," the forerunner of the modern "flume," and this was one of the major attractions. During the early years of the twentieth century, a number of well-built cottages began to appear. D. Russell Brown, a wealthy Providence businessman who had been governor from 1892 to 1895, led the way for the real estate development of the area.

The beach was well maintained and many enjoyed bathing at Front Beach and Brush Neck Cove. Bathing was still not popular, as many had fears that total immersion in water was harmful. For those who dared, however, there were bathing suits suitable for wearing at the shore. They were one-piece suits, with sleeves, which reached to the knees. The women's suits also had skirts.

Warwick's shore line, now easily accessible by trolley, offered attractions for all, from the mill workers to the very wealthy. While the trains, steamboats, and trolleys were bringing many to Warwick's amusement parks, they were also taking tourists to Warwick's campgrounds. Long noted for its summer hotels and tourist homes, Warwick also became famous for its summer campgrounds. One of these was the Cole Camp, located between present-day Hoxsie Four Corners and Conimicut Village.

Warwick historian Henry A.L. Brown, in "Occupastuxet to Red Bank: A History of the Cole Farm," traced the history of the campground from the late nineteenth century until its close in 1967. The site of the camp, Brown explained, was on the historic property that once belonged to the Greene family. The house, which stood there in the early twentieth century, was built in 1676 and was the birthplace of the Revolutionary War hero Christopher Greene. The Greene family held their family reunions on the property and many famous guests, including Benjamin Franklin, came to visit.

In 1823, the property was purchased by the Cole family. The Greenes had begun a tradition of planting elm trees on the property and the Coles continued this practice, naming their farm "The Elms." The Coles were soon famous for their clambakes, especially for those held on Saturday. This was the time when the camp was reserved for about 50 of Providence's most affluent citizens. They called themselves the "Saturday Club" and became well known for their lavish entertainments. Both Governor William Sprague and General Ambrose Burnside were members, and they invited many Northern generals and influential politicians to the clambakes. Eliza Cole, in 1900, noted, "In those days we used to put in clams, oysters, mussels, lobsters, fish, chickens, and corn all in one bake." In time, the Coles allowed guests to have the use of the farm, and campers began pitching tents there and staying for the weekend. As it was conveniently located on the Buttonwoods–Oakland Beach trolley line, it became a favorite spot for campers, who were charged a small fee for tenting and were able to buy produce from the farm.

One of the most serious hazards of the early twentieth century was fire. From 1891 until the formation of the Warwick Firemen's League in 1926, major fires in the town brought about the creation of a number of fire departments. In 1891, after a very serious blaze that destroyed a large part of the Cranston section of Pawtuxet Village, Volunteer Fire Company No. 1, Pawtuxet, was incorporated and purchased a hand engine called "Fire King." Within a year, the hand engine and the new company gained fame and made the cause for fire companies more popular when they played a key role in a Pawtuxet fire that threatened to destroy the village. Fighting that blaze, the volunteers quickly dropped the engine's suction pump into one of the deepest areas at the Cranston side of the Pawtuxet River dam and quickly had a steady stream playing on the burning buildings.

The first two decades of the twentieth century saw a series of fires at Rocky Point, Oakland Beach, Potowomut, and Apponaug. In 1903, fire destroyed the Oakland Beach Hotel, which was built in 1874 at a cost of $100,000. In addition, the flames took the hotel stable, icehouse, and Hope Cottage. Newspaper accounts at the time noted the following:

> The flames burned with great rapidity . . . and within a few minutes the structure was a mass of fire against which nothing at hand could cope. . . . In fact there was nothing at Oakland Beach with which to fight the fire, the only quantity of water being in a large tank on the roof of the hotel building which could not be reached and which soon was licked up by the devouring element.

In 1918, employees of the George Dean Company gathered in front of the Kentish Armory en route to an outlying area along the shore. (Courtesy Phyllis Dean Collection.)

A volunteer bucket brigade worked to save surrounding cottages and was successful when the wind finally died down. Another fire at Oakland Beach in 1916 destroyed the old post office, general store, barbershop, bowling alleys, and moving picture theater.

In 1906, Rocky Point suffered again in a series of devastating fires. In the 1890s, the Rocky Point hotel, ice cream parlor, and shore dinner hall had been totally destroyed, as there was no fire apparatus to aid in putting out the blaze. Once again, in 1906, it was reported that "There were no means at hand with which to combat the flames." Buckets of water were the only means available and, as there was a shortage of men on hand to man the buckets, women from the area rushed to the scene and volunteered their services. Colonel R.A. Harrington, in true showmanship style, accepted the loss and "genially added that he will charge his patrons nothing extra for a view of the ruins."

In 1909, the magnificent Colonel William Goddard Mansion at Potowomut was destroyed and there was no means of fighting the fire. Help came to man the fire buckets and many of the farmhands at the estate braved the flames to enter the house to save some of the valuable works of art. Within two hours after the fire broke out, the mansion was nothing but a smoldering ruin. In 1910, a devastating fire destroyed a large section of Beach Avenue in Conimicut and, once again, there was no available means of fighting the fire except bucket brigades.

As a result of these and other fires, communities began to support volunteer fire companies. In addition to the Apponaug, Lakewood, and Pawtuxet Fire Companies, which were organized before the end of the nineteenth century, five additional volunteer fire companies came into existence. The Norwood Company was organized in 1908 and purchased a chemical truck as its first piece of apparatus. In Conimicut, in 1911, 36 men

Before the devastating fire of 1911, these wooden structures, the Kentish Artillery Armory and St. Barnabas' Church, were part of Apponaug's community life. Both buildings have been replaced.

became charter members of the Conimicut Volunteer Company and purchased a hand-drawn truck. Oakland Beach organized a fire company in 1913 and, in 1917, purchased an American LaFrance truck with a pumping capacity of 250 gallons per minute. This was the first motorized pumping engine in the town. Bayside organized a fire company in 1915, and the Greenwood Company came into being in 1924.

The town began to support these companies by voting an appropriation of $100 to each of the four Warwick companies in 1913, and $75 to the Pawtuxet Volunteers. In 1924, the town appropriated $7,000 for the benefit of the various fire departments.

Even with the efforts of the volunteer fire departments, Warwick was severely crippled by fire during the early part of the century. One of the worst was in Apponaug in 1911. This fire destroyed both St. Barnabas' Church and the Kentish Artillery Armory. The blaze, it is believed, started in an outbuilding at the rear of the armory. It was a cold night in March and it seems that a tramp entered the building to keep warm, and to find his way, he lit matches, which ignited some papers in the building.

A watchman at the Apponaug Print Works spotted the blaze and sent out the alarm that was quickly answered by the Apponaug Volunteers. Unfortunately, there was a very weak water supply and only one line was operable at a time. In addition it was bitter cold, about 18 degrees, and the water froze as soon as it hit the buildings. Fortunately, the firefighters were able to keep the fire from spreading throughout Apponaug.

The years 1914 and 1915 were especially severe for fires in Warwick. In 1914, Rocky Point was again the scene of a serious blaze as six buildings were destroyed. The Conimicut Volunteer Company quickly responded and, despite being hampered by falling electric wires, was able to save a number of buildings on the amusement park's Midway.

In April 1915, fire destroyed the stable, laundry, garage, boiler room, and part of the observation tower at Senator Nelson W. Aldrich's estate. The damage was estimated at $300,000. Lines were connected to a system in the water tower, but the pressure was so weak that it did little to help fight the blaze. Even at this late date, only a small section of Warwick had a modern water supply system. Ironically, the question of making provision for the installation of an adequate water service in the town of Warwick was discussed at the financial town meeting during that day and the taxpayers had voted against the proposition.

The dawning of the twentieth century saw the political clamor for more services for the western mill villages in Warwick intensify into a demand for separation. On March 14, 1913, Governor Aram Pothier signed a bill into law which divided Warwick by taking the third, fourth, and fifth representative districts to make West Warwick a separate town. The act that accomplished this was introduced and nurtured by Walter G. Hartford after similar bills, introduced by Frank Woodmansee in 1910 and Walter C. Gardner in 1912, had failed to receive favorable action. While success finally came in 1913, agitation for this division, which took 8.3 square miles from Warwick to make the western section of the town an independent entity, had started at least a half-century earlier.

For many years, talk of separation was quickly stifled by Charles R. Brayton, the "blind boss," who ruled the state with very little opposition for many years. In much the same manner, Brayton's counterpart in Warwick, Webster Knight, ruled the town with an iron hand. As the senior partner of the B.B.&R. Knight Co., Webster Knight exerted a

Volunteer firefighting companies played an essential role in the early twentieth century. The Vigilant Fire Company of Apponaug had their own band and participated in the many parades of the times, c. 1921. (Courtesy Charles Pendergast Collection.)

tremendous influence on the mill villages and controlled a sizable number of votes. He was elected to the Warwick Town Council and became its president from 1893 to 1898.

At the turn of the century, the abuses of boss rule were challenged on both the state and local levels. In 1907, even Nelson W. Aldrich, who was the chief benefactor, protested against Brayton's despotic rule. The feeling that the "old boss," now going blind, could be ousted from power caused his enemies to attempt to destroy his control. Brayton surprised everyone by fighting back and keeping his control over the state senate. This was his power base and he wasn't going to allow the creation of a new town that would be Democratic. The fight continued, however, and the "progressive" branch of the Republican Party was beginning to demand sweeping reforms and was willing to challenge the "machine" politics of Brayton and other "bosses."

In Warwick, the discontent of both Democrats and reform-minded Republicans was directed at Webster "Boss" Knight. The two factions joined to form a Citizens Party. They labeled Knight "the autocrat of the council table" and accused him of using his position to serve his firm rather than the citizens of Warwick.

Two of the key figures in leading the fight for separation were Walter G. Hartford and Patrick Henry Quinn. Hartford took the initiative and formed the Warwick Division Club, made up of some of the town's leading citizens. He called for a general referendum on the issue and even offered to pay for the cost. In 1913, Hartford defeated Warwick senator Walter A. Bowen on the single issue of dividing the town, and the state legislature, no longer controlled by Brayton who had died in 1910, was willing to move in that direction.

While Hartford's work in the legislature brought about the division, it was made possible only through the political maneuvering of the brilliant lawyer Patrick H. Quinn, the son of an Irish immigrant. P.H. Quinn's record in the late nineteenth and early twentieth centuries was truly impressive. In 1898, he was elected secretary to the Democratic State Central Committee and later became its chairman. For ten years he also served as chairman of the Warwick Democratic Town Committee. In 1899, despite the fact that he was a Democrat, he was named town solicitor.

Quinn's control over the financial town meeting was the key in bringing the pressure to bear for a division of Warwick. When he discovered, in 1908, that the Republican town treasurer Herbert W. Barber, acting on Republican Town Council recommendations, was paying each council member $200 per year rather than the $50 voted at the town's financial meeting, Quinn took positive action. He brought suit in Superior Court and eventually in the Supreme Court where, in the case of *Quinn v. Barber, Town Treasurer*, an injunction was granted against Barber. This was a major breakthrough for the cause of separation and indicated that it was possible to win a case against the firmly entrenched establishment.

Quinn and Hartford were rewarded for their efforts in 1913, when the Republican General Assembly granted permission for Warwick to be divided, and incorporated West Warwick as a town. The Republican governor at the time, Aram Pothier, appointed Walter A. Hartford, Charles A. Wilson, William P. Sheffield, Oliver A. Langevin, and Patrick Henry Quinn to a five-man commission to complete the process of separation.

As a result of the 1913 division of Warwick, the high school went to West Warwick and the Apponaug Grammar School became the Warwick High School until it burned in 1927. (Courtesy Dorothy Mayor Collection.)

In 1913, when the town was divided, Warwick's municipal assets were divided as equally as possible. Of the two major assets, West Warwick received the high school, Warwick kept the Town Hall. Other assets were carefully appraised and divided even to the stationery supplies on hand. When it came to the question of the town debt, West Warwick assumed a debt of $300,000 and Warwick's share was determined to be $224,114. Both bonds were retired on July 1, 1944.

When Warwick ceded the 8.3 square miles to the new town of West Warwick, she lost the mill villages of Crompton, Centerville, Arctic, Riverpoint, Clyde, Phenix, and a large portion of Natick. With these villages gone, Warwick's industrial base was centered around the important mill villages of Pontiac, Hillsgrove, and Apponaug. The old town went from a population of over 26,000 to 13,000 and lost three of her five representatives in the General Assembly.

In addition to losing the industrial area, the stores, shops, and theaters were gone as well. Two of the largest retail stores at the time were the Star Clothing House (St. Onge) and Sinnott's Clothing Store in Arctic. While most of Warwick's mill workers and farmers wore simple and durable garments, businessmen and the more affluent were going to Providence or Arctic to get the latest styles. Suits in Arctic sold for as little as $9; derbies, fedoras, and straw hats, for a dollar or two; and shoes for men and women could be bought for two or three dollars.

While men's suits tended to be conventional and mostly black, brown, and gray, women's fashions were becoming more daring for those who could afford it. Women wore very large hats and "hobble" skirts, which were often so narrow that walking was difficult. Lace garments were coming into vogue and, for those who dared, there were V-neck blouses, commonly called "pneumonia" blouses.

111

By mutual agreement, when the high school went to the new town, the Warwick students in the Class of 1913 were allowed to graduate as scheduled. They had already paid their senior dues of 15¢ per month and were entitled to the senior banquet, prom, and graduation. The only hall large enough at the time to accommodate the large crowd that gathered was Thornton's Theatre, then known as the "Opera House," in Clyde.

Despite the split, the young men of West Warwick headed for Rocky Point on the trolleys every Saturday night and, as former governor Robert E. Quinn observed in a 1963 interview, "Friday night was band concert night at Arctic, Phenix, and Crompton. The crowds were so large that it was impossible to walk on the sidewalks." During the summer people were flocking to Rocky Point to enjoy dining at the Shore Dinner hall, which was out over the water and supported by pilings. Those very fortunate ones, such as Joseph Fitzpatrick's family, were able to spend the summer at the Rocky Beach campgrounds when a season's rental was about $25.

Joe Fitzpatrick, who later was the stage manager at the theater at Rocky Point, recalled that Rocky Point Theatre had five dressing rooms for its performers and many of the top vaudeville stars performed at the park. Rocky Point was able to take advantage of the Providence ordinance that barred vaudeville in that city on Sundays. Top-name acts on the Keith circuit, which came to Providence's Keith-Albee Theatre, played at Rocky Point, as Warwick had no such ordinance.

In the years preceding World War I, the motion pictures were beginning to come into their own. As Rocky Point usually had the newest films, people came from miles around. It was not uncommon for chauffeur-driven Rolls Royce or Packard limousines to drive up with their passengers on a regular basis. Admission was 10¢, but the best seats in the center aisle cost an additional nickel.

In the first two decades of the twentieth century there were still many more horses and carriages than there were automobiles, but the trend towards the motorcar was sure and steady. The first automobile in the area was in 1898, and it was a steam-powered car. By 1901, an electric "truck" was already making deliveries in Providence, and by 1920, the gasoline-powered automobile was here to stay. From less than 800 automobiles registered in Rhode Island in 1900, the number had grown to well over 40,000 by 1920. This meant an increased popularity of Warwick as a resort area and, as a result, the communities of Lakewood and Pawtuxet grew as suburban entities.

While much of Warwick was farmland, the mill villages of Apponaug, Pontiac, and Hillsgrove were very important and Warwick's prosperity depended upon them. After a number of difficult years when production nearly ceased, the Apponaug Bleaching, Dyeing, and Print Works Co. concentrated on the printing of staple cotton fabrics and enjoyed a limited success until 1913, when, under the leadership of J.P. Farnsworth, it made a major change and began a period of unprecedented prosperity.

Farnsworth and his colleagues decided to direct the company toward the development of finishing processes for fine textiles instead of staple fabrics. This field, which eventually included the finer grades of cotton, rayon, Celanese, and mixed fabrics, required a greater technical skill and more delicate workmanship. Fortunately, the company was able to acquire the skills of Alfred L. Lustig, one of the world's foremost color chemists. In 1913, after a brilliant career as a chemist, he was persuaded to come to Apponaug as the general manager of the Apponaug Company. In 1917, when J.P. Farnsworth died, Lustig was made the president of the company. Under Lustig's leadership, the Apponaug plant became a major employer in Warwick, attracting skilled workers from nearby Natick, Clyde, and Riverpoint.

A complete transition, from vaudeville to the "silent movies" to the "talkies," took place in Warwick in less than 20 years. This rapid change came against a background of drastic departures from the lifestyle enjoyed in the nineteenth-century mill villages. During this time, Warwick residents were thrust into a world far different from that of their fathers. Among the many political and economic changes they witnessed was a major war, involving nearly every country in the Western world. The use of telephones, which were now extended into the town, combined with a higher literacy rate, helped to make townsmen more aware of national and world events.

The great optimism, patriotism, and altruism, spurred on by President Wilson's eloquent pleas to fight the "war to end all wars" and "make the world safe for democracy," prompted large numbers of volunteers from Warwick and the Pawtuxet Valley to join the more than 28,000 Rhode Island troops when America entered the war. Apponaug historian Dorothy Mayor, referring to the Apponaug train station in her booklet, "I Remember Apponaug," noted the following:

> During World War I a temporary encampment was set up in the freight yard. It was exciting to watch the sentries march back and forth, to listen to the bugle calls, and to be present when a troop train stopped to take the boys to Boston on the first leg of their journey to France.

Many mill workers, feeling great sympathy for Italy and France, enlisted in the 11th Company, Coast Artillery Corps of the Rhode Island National Guard. In July 1918, they

During World War I, large numbers of troops departed from Apponaug Station, an important link between Boston and New York. (Courtesy Dorothy Mayor Collection.)

Patriotism ran high during World War I and crowds such as these often met at bond rallies at the Town Hall. (Courtesy Dorothy Mayor Collection.)

were inducted into Federal Service and some were assigned to the Headquarters Co. of the 66th Regiment, Field Artillery. Because of their fluency in French, coupled with obvious intelligence, workers who held only the most menial jobs in the mills now found themselves in positions of responsibility and command.

Unfortunately, the enthusiasm and patriotism once felt by Rhode Islanders turned to bitter cynicism by the 1920s. Warwick citizens, predominantly pro-French and pro-Ally, were bitterly disappointed with the inadequate Treaty of Versailles, which saw the nation's fondest dreams shattered as the European countries sought revenge and "divided the spoils" of war.

While there was some prosperity in the textile industry as a result of the war, many returning soldiers were no longer content with life in the paternalistic villages. In 1919, the Knight family sold their fabulous empire to the Consolidated Textile Corporation of New York for a reported $20,000,000, and within a year, the prosperity that followed World War I disappeared.

The poor foreign policies of President Warren G. Harding's administration, coupled with the failure of Rhode Island manufacturers to improve and update their holdings, saw the beginning of the end of the once predominant textile industry along the Pawtuxet River.

In addition, many residents were stunned by the passage of the 18th Amendment in January 1919, which prohibited "the manufacture, sale or transportation" of intoxicating beverages. There was disbelief, disappointment, and a sense of being deprived of a liberty of conscience and free will. At first, many scoffed at the amendment and compared it with earlier temperance movements fostered by mill owners such as Enos Lapham. When it became obvious that every state but Rhode Island and Connecticut ratified the amendment, the disbelief turned to anger. Then, on October 28, 1919, the Volstead Act was passed. It defined intoxicating beverages as "those containing over one-half of one percent alcohol" and set January 1, 1920, as the date when sales would become illegal.

Even those who didn't use, or favor, alcoholic beverages feared the new law would seriously curtail business by greatly diminishing the crowds that came to Rocky Point and Oakland Beach to drink and be entertained. Others, having some experience with the "back-rooms" of restaurants in "dry" states, believed sections of Warwick, already notorious for their bars, saloons, shows, and "fast-houses," would see an increase in illegal activities and drive the better hotels and restaurants from the scene.

Unfortunately, as the 1920s progressed, many of the fears were well founded. Warwick never did become "dry" in reality, and it would appear that if all 1,520 federal agents hired to enforce the Volstead Act were stationed in the Pawtuxet Valley, the flow of liquor would still have continued uninhibited. Warwick, as many other cities and towns in Rhode Island, became infamous for smuggling and bootlegging. In addition, Warwick, with its many speakeasies in Oakland Beach, Pawtuxet, and Apponaug, gained the reputation of being a "wide-open" town.

As might well be expected, the 18th Amendment gave organized crime a foothold in Warwick. When the notorious "Rettich gang" was exposed on Warwick Neck, many Warwick and West Warwick connections were mentioned. It was generally believed that the *Black Duck*, a "rum-running" speedboat, was the property of one of Arctic's hotel and bar owners. When the Coast Guard riddled the boat with machine-gun fire and killed three of the crew on December 29, 1930, there was a great deal of indignation in Warwick.

Many of the town's senior citizens can recall when cars bearing Massachusetts and Connecticut license plates, as well as those of Rhode Island, were often seen parked at Oakland Beach or at the Hill House in Greenwood or at many of Warwick's other obvious "speakeasies." In a number of "restaurants," wires and alarms were strung to warn of raids from the "feds" and also from rival "gangs." Observers of the times commented that often before the raids occurred in the morning, trucks were seen carting off the illegal goods from Warwick. They also noted that by 6 p.m. the "speakeasies" were again open for business.

What many find more amazing than the ease of obtaining alcoholic beverages is the fact that it was so easily accepted and that, with the possible exception of Warwick Neck's Rettich gang, no widespread violence or "gang-wars" occurred. Apparently, the fear was there, as some bar owners hired bodyguards, and intricate alarm systems were installed in some speakeasies, but no reported incidents of any magnitude appear. One old-timer has explained it in this fashion, "Everyone knew what he could do. Some ran bars, hotels and restaurants with liquor, some didn't. 'One-armed bandits' [slot machines] were given to some, and others were allowed to run card games and numbers. We all cooperated."

Prohibition, so often glorified in the movies of the 1930s and the 1940s, was relatively short lived and, in reality, was only one small part of the many more important and exciting changes that took place in the twenties. While Warwick's young men were serving in Europe, the textile industry boomed in Pontiac, Apponaug, and Natick as war contracts brought the factories in the Pawtuxet Valley to full production.

When the war ended, many veterans returned home determined to exercise their rights as citizens. Veterans of all ethnic groups now had a common bond and united to vie for mutual benefits and to defeat "native American" movements. Further optimism came when women received the right to vote in 1917. The end of "bossism" and corruption seemed to be at hand. While Warwick was attempting to adjust to the changes brought about by Prohibition and by the Knight family selling their interests in the textiles, adverse conditions battered the area. In 1918–1919, a very severe winter, in which trolley lines were tied up and people were isolated, was followed by an influenza epidemic that especially affected those in the mill villages.

In January 1922, the era of paternalism rapidly came to a close as Warwick encountered one of the area's longest and most devastating strikes. Before the eight-month walkout ended, there was widespread turmoil and suffering throughout the Pawtuxet Valley. Mills closed, nearly 5,000 workers were idle, breadlines formed, armed soldiers patrolled the villages, and nearly all business activity ceased.

Warwick no longer lived under the illusion that the prosperous period that followed World War I would continue. When Webster Knight and his brother, C. Prescott, sold their mills to the Consolidated Textile Corporation, the new owners purchased the B.B.&R. Knight name and the "Fruit of the Loom" trademark, hoping to continue to enjoy the same high profits as had the Knights.

Almost immediately, however, they found this was not going to occur as they began to suffer the losses of a declining market and competition from the South and from Europe. The attempt was made to lower prices, to increase the demand for the product, and to eliminate competition. In 1921, to cut costs, the company lowered wages by 22.5 percent and increased the number of hours operatives were required to work per week. Matters became worse when, on January 20, 1922, the Goddard Brothers and the owners of the B.B.&R. Knight Company were going to cut wages an additional 20 to 22 percent. Nearly all mill villages were soon affected by the cuts.

On January 21, 1922, 250 weavers at the Royal Mill in Riverpoint and workers in the Natick and Pontiac mills declared a strike. The Valley Queen Mill in Riverpoint, now the Bradford Soap Works, closed and sympathy strikes took place in other mills in the Pawtuxet Valley. Large numbers of strikers from the Knight mills in Natick and Riverpoint began going from mill to mill urging their fellow workers to leave their positions. News of the walkout dominated the front page, even overshadowing the reports of the death of Pope Benedict XV and of three cases of smallpox in Warwick.

As was feared, violence was inevitable. Rioting erupted on January 31, 1922, at the Natick mill. Police from Warwick, West Warwick, and Coventry were called out to quell the disturbance, which began when an alleged rioter was arrested. The mob began smashing windows and throwing stones at the mill, and the situation was rapidly getting out of control. Finally, the striker was released and the rioting subsided.

For the next few days, many in Warwick and other mill villages in the Pawtuxet Valley lived under the shadow of violence and retaliation. Without wages, many workers were faced with severe economic repercussions. Those who lived in company houses were threatened with eviction, and the unions opened cafeterias to help feed the destitute. Hopes for an early settlement were dashed on February 1 when workers asked for the restoration of wage cuts with a 48-hour week and management refused.

116

In the early 1920s, the Rhode Island Militia Brigade enjoyed an outing at Oakland Beach. The beach's many amusement rides were later destroyed by the Hurricane of 1938. (Courtesy Henry A.L. Brown Collection.)

On the following day, over 300 strikers marched to Apponaug and, with the aid of a cornet and a bass drum, sent up such a din that soon nearly all the operatives at the Apponaug Mill walked out, crippling the plant and forcing it to cease operations. During the following week, violence again erupted. Fights, rock throwing, and other forms of violence halted operations.

The strike did irreparable damage to both the mills and the mill villages in Warwick. When the strike finally came to an end, the paternalistic relationship of mill owner and workers had disintegrated and the textile industry no longer ruled supreme in Rhode Island. Before the strike was over, there was a great deal of violence, bitterness, and hardship inflicted on both strikers and management.

Mill owners believed that calling out the state's militia would bring an immediate end to the strike. Political pressure was exerted upon Governor Emory J. San Souci to order the troops to the Pawtuxet Valley to protect the mills and force the strikers back to work. San Souci, stunned by the turn of events, bowed to the wishes of the mill owners and sent the Mounted Command of the National Guard to the villages of Pontiac and Natick. Over 150 troops, many of them on horseback, arrived at Brown Square in Natick to stop a riot at the mill during the last week in February 1922.

For a very short time it appeared that Rhode Island would be faced with its most serious rebellion when over 1,000 men, women, and children gathered to face the troops in Natick. A *Pawtuxet Valley Daily Times* article, written in 1963, relates that "Father Tirrocchi of St. Joseph's Church came running out of the rectory and pleaded with the crowd in Italian to go home and avoid bloodshed." His plea was heeded and the crowd disappeared from the square, allowing the troops to turn their attention to the rioting at the mill. A machine gun was mounted on the roof of the Natick Mill and National Guardsmen manned the weapon and patrolled the streets.

117

Finally, on September 12, 1922, the owners of the B.B.&R. Knight Company, the Crompton Company, the Hope Company, and the Interlaken Mills all agreed to restore the wage scale that was in effect before January 1922. William McLoughlin, in his *Rhode Island: A History*, stated, "Their willingness to agree was in part dictated by the end of the recession and the upsurge of production orders. But the workers had at last learned that they could succeed. . . . Employers claimed that the unions were cutting the throats of the workers by cutting the profits of the owners. But in truth, the day of New England's supremacy in the textile industry was over."

During the twenties, Warwick nearly doubled in population as it went from 13,481 in 1920 to 23,196 at the end of the decade. Warwick was a town of dramatic contrasts as it became home for some of Rhode Island's most affluent and most destitute citizens. This period of prohibition, gangsterism, high stock market profits, strikes, and flamboyant political campaigns saw Warwick's fire and police personnel at times acting more like comic vaudeville actors than public servants, and, at the same time, these people were struggling to make progress towards creating real and significant police and fire departments.

For the very wealthy, the fine estates along the Cowesett shore and Warwick Neck vied with those at Newport, Jamestown, and Watch Hill for opulence and glamour. Beautiful automobiles, including Pierce Arrows and Marmons, as well as Cadillacs, Packards, and Lincolns, driven often by Irish chauffeurs, elegantly proceeded up blue-stone or oyster-shell driveways to multi-roomed mansions.

Many of the fine Victorian houses at Warwick Neck had rooms large enough for dancing and large soirees. Those who didn't come by auto could get there by trolley and

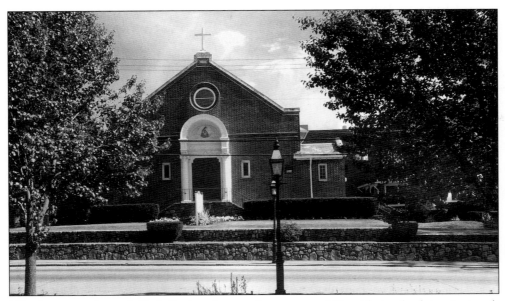

The large numbers of Catholic immigrants that came to Warwick in the late nineteenth century and early twentieth centuries provided the impetus for the building of St. Catherine's Church in Apponaug. Construction was halted during World War I and completed in 1919.

take a taxi to their destination. Most of the Irish maids and Italian gardeners who took care of the houses and grounds, however, usually walked from the trolley stop, and while the employers spent vast amounts on food, liquor, and pleasure vehicles, these servants were among the lowest paid workers in the state.

Many of the large estates were actually farms. On the Kirby estate alone, there were 200 cattle and 1,500 turkeys. Other estates in Warwick were also interested in raising purebred sheep, prize cattle, and horses. As the decade wore on, however, the increased interest in yachting brought about a Warwick Neck Country Club. By 1927, 55 yachts were registered at the club and an excellent golf course and tennis court were built. The prosperity of the twenties was very obvious on the Neck as new and fabulous inventions made life easy and luxurious.

While members of the Warwick Neck Country Club were discussing the merits of the Bristol-made Herreshoff racing yachts and their most recent successes on the stock market, others on the Neck, such as Carl Rettich and his friends, were inquiring about adding layers of telephone directories for "armour-plating" and triple Liberty airplane engines to their sleek speedboats. The only races they were interested in winning were the ones with the Coast Guard, for these people represented the rum-runners and the bootleggers who found Warwick's many coves and inlets ideal locations for their illegal activities.

Warwick Neck was also the center of political activity as the very wealthy Peter G. Gerry, using his Warwick Neck address, successfully ran for the U.S. Senate. Gerry, whose great wealth made him a leader of the Democratic Party, often found himself at odds with the rank and file members. For a number of years, a behind-the-scenes struggle for supremacy in the party was carried on between Gerry and Theodore Francis Green.

For a brief period in the 1920s, the Democratic Party began to make giant strides on a state level against the well-entrenched Republicans. In Warwick, large numbers of first- and second-generation descendants of immigrants began to forego ethnic rivalries and unite. Feeling betrayed by the Republicans in the strike of 1922, the mill workers helped put Democrat William S. Flynn in as governor, Felix Toupin as lieutenant governor, and elected large numbers to the General Assembly. While they did not control the state legislature, Democrats found that their numbers were large enough to frustrate Republican legislation.

Unfortunately, the standard of living in Warwick's mill villages and on the small farms was much lower than that of the middle class. In 1920, the average wage in the textile industry was a little over 18¢ per hour and, while it did rise to 40¢ by the end of the decade, there were many unemployed and without any income. The exception to much of the decline of the textile industry was the Apponaug Company, which found itself the recipient of increased business. To keep pace with major changes and innovations, the plant, under Lustig, underwent a major modernization between 1920 and 1928, a time when other mills were talking of closing.

After the strike of 1922, many laborers found it difficult to find work and to afford even the meager lifestyle to which they had become accustomed. In addition, the Ku Klux Klan grew in the state. Klansmen met in Pawtuxet, openly walked through Rocky Point, and burned crosses in the fields near Hardig Brook. In Rhode Island, they were more anti-Catholic than anti-black and their presence was ominous. More subtle forms of discrimination, such as the variety of jobs open for certain groups, the denial of membership to certain organizations, and other indications of prejudice, loomed large in Warwick as it did in other areas of Rhode Island.

During the twenties, mass-produced automobiles became plentiful and, in 1921, Rhode Island reported there were over 40,000 vehicles. The "go anywhere vehicle" was soon making its way into Warwick and brought about a number of problems. One, in a humorous light, occurred when Sergeant Joseph Ricketts, an early member of Warwick's police force, had to write a ticket for a motorist speeding through Apponaug's Four Corners. There were no motor vehicle violation laws in Warwick at the time, so the officer charged the driver with "assault with a dangerous weapon."

The twenties also brought about a closer look at the methods of law enforcement and a serious attempt for improvement. While constables were appointed as early as 1648 to help keep the peace, it wasn't until the nineteenth century that changes began to occur in the town. By the twentieth century, sheriffs and deputy sheriffs were given the job of keeping the peace and directing the constables in the various towns. As early as 1906, Warwick had a chief of police, Theodore S. Andrews, and voted to pay him $500 per year. There were also four police stations, and officers were placed in charge of each. Not only was the job considered a minor one, but many of the officers were janitors of the buildings as well. In 1913, the General Laws of the State of Rhode Island required "Police Commissioners" in the various municipalities, and Warwick came closer to having a force which consisted of more than "special constables" at Rocky Point or at the mills.

Anne Crawford Allen Holst, one of Warwick's most meticulous historians, noted in 1916 that "young fellows in Apponaug were chanting a sort of folk song" that went as follows:

> Oh, you can't stand on the sidewalk,
> you can't stand in the street, you can't stand under the
> LEK'tric light when Owen's on the beat.

Mrs. Holst stated that the use of the word "beat" infers a regular patrol and that the Owen referred to was Owen Lynch, one of the sons of Michael B. Lynch of Apponaug, the man who was high sheriff of Kent County from 1902 until he retired in 1929. The remarkable sheriff was given the job of coordinating the Warwick, West Warwick, and Coventry police chiefs and their constables during the strike of 1922. Lynch was 78 years old at the time and was given a great deal of praise for doing an outstanding job. He relied heavily on Theodore Andrews of Warwick, his deputy who later succeeded him as high sheriff. During the early part of the century, Andrews was the chief of police in Warwick.

The *Warwick City Times*, a short-lived local paper in the 1930s, placed the first permanent police force in 1921. The paper recorded that the chief was Ellis A. Cranston and noted that James G. Ludlow, a local blacksmith, and Henry Ledoux, were among the first permanent patrolmen. The *Times* asserted that there "was no day patrolman then and only six men were on duty at night." Ledoux, who succeeded Cranston, was Warwick's first motorcycle "cop."

Automobile accidents always drew large crowds. H.H. Rogers Jr. managed to catch the action at the Greenwood Bridge in 1915. (Courtesy Dave Matteson Collection.)

Cranston who, according to the *Times*, was best remembered for his political influence, realized the necessity of having men on his force that could speak the language of the immigrants. Because of the ever-increasing numbers of Italians in Pontiac and Natick, Cranston hired Albert N. Izzi as a special constable in 1919. Later, Izzi became part of the small permanent force. The force had no regular uniforms at the time, and Izzi, who had played saxophone in the Natick band, wore his band uniform for a number of years.

Forrest Sprague, one of Warwick's best-known and respected police chiefs, also joined the force in the 1920s. He recalled that, at the time, there were no police cars; officers had to use their own, and there was a "lot of nothing" between the villages. The Warwick newspaper charged that Chief Cranston was lax and that visitors to the police station, which was in the basement of the Town Hall, often found the police officers "playing cards." They also charged that Cranston's records were poorly kept and that when Ledoux took over in 1930, he closed over 100 speakeasies.

During this period, the fire companies in Warwick were just coming into their own. As strange as it may seem today, there was a great deal of rivalry between companies and disputes over which company had jurisdiction at the fire. On a few occasions, fistfights broke out among the rival firefighters as the buildings burned.

Two very significant fires took a great toll in Apponaug. One, in 1922, destroyed Norton's garage, south of Apponaug's Four Corners, and then spread to the Warwick Lumber Company and four dwelling houses. Damaged by the fire in the garage, ten automobiles and an assortment of tools and supplies were ruined. In addition to the Apponaug Volunteers, the Warwick police were called to aid in directing traffic, and soon all other Warwick fire companies came to help. By this time, 100 hydrants had been installed in Warwick and all those in Apponaug were put in use.

Seen here in front of the Apponaug Hotel, the "Green Hornet" bus was a familiar site at Apponaug's Four Corners in the 1920s. (Courtesy Charles Arthur Moore II Collection.)

In 1924, all Warwick firefighters again cooperated in an attempt to quell the flames at the Apponaug Grammar School, which after the 1913 separation had become the Warwick High School. In 1924, a devastating fire in Conimicut destroyed two blocks on West Shore Road and ruined seven stores. As a result of these fires and the obvious advantages of cooperation between the departments, the Warwick Firemen's League was created in 1926. By this time, the Greenwood Fire Company had been organized (1924), bringing the total companies to seven. At their meeting, the fire companies succeeded in setting up district lines, outlining procedures for cooperation at major fires, and establishing the scope and authority of fire chiefs in a variety of instances. By the end of the decade, Warwick was successful in installing a water system that served much of the town.

While the wealthy sailed their yachts or drove their expensive cars to escape the cares of the times, the less affluent sought escape at the shore resorts and amusement centers. After Randall Harrington died, Paul and Alfred Castiglioni assumed control of Rocky Point. During their tenure, a number of new attractions were added to the Midway and thousands flooded the park. Admission was free and families could determine what they could spend, as each ride charged a fee. Big attractions in the thirties included appearances by Gertrude C. Ederle, who swam the English Channel in 1926, and by the "Sultan of Swat," Babe Ruth. Edward Gillan McGuire was the well-known "barker" at the Midway and later became a very famous magician called "The Great Gillan."

Oakland Beach fared well also. In 1919, Joseph Carrolo witnessed the impact of the large numbers who came to the beach by trolley, and he formed the Oakland Beach Association, which turned the beach into a major amusement center. A full-sized roller coaster, owned by the Sholes family, along with a number of other rides, was brought in by the association. For the next decade, Oakland Beach enjoyed a period of great prosperity.

7. Warwick from 1930 to 1950

From 1930 until the outbreak of World War II in 1941, Warwick went through a period that balanced difficulties and tragedies with excitement and pleasure. Many of the problems encountered were due to the poor economic conditions and to the devastating effects of the Hurricane of 1938. Even before the Stock Market Crash of 1929, Warwick was struggling with serious economic difficulties brought about by the failure of the textile industry. The giant B.B.&R. Knight Company, with mills in Pontiac and Natick, tried desperately to cut costs by the "speed-up" system, where employees were urged to work faster, and the "stretch-out" policy, which used fewer workers to reach the same production quotas. These attempts failed and textile mills in Warwick and West Warwick closed, leaving many unemployed.

By 1930, 27 percent of those engaged in cotton textile manufacturing and 24 percent of those in the woolen industry in Rhode Island were out of jobs. The resulting economic depression was felt most acutely by the immigrant workers in the mill villages.

The major exception to the declining textile industry was the Apponaug Company, which specialized in developing superior methods of bleaching, dyeing, and printing textiles. The company was also one of the first to enter into the field of synthetic fabrics and, by 1934, was the first in America to produce "wash and wear" no iron fabrics. The Apponaug plant became a major employer in Warwick, attracting skilled workers from nearby Pontiac and Natick, as well as other sections of Warwick. The economic impact of the mills in Apponaug continued well into the twentieth century. For nearly four decades, the Apponaug Company was Warwick's largest employer and was instrumental in many of the changes that took place in Warwick.

The influence of the mill extended well beyond the salaries paid to workers in the sprawling complex, for the prosperity of the mill meant prosperity for the village. Most businesses in Apponaug would not have survived had the mill closed its doors.

Warwick elected to become a city in 1931. The town's population had grown to over 23,000 and no longer could be considered a small town. Within Warwick's 36.26 square miles of land, there were many miles of water mains, over 100 miles of accepted highways, several hundred town employees, more than 6,000 families, and 21 school buildings. Political leaders were becoming very much aware that the eighteenth- and nineteenth-century form of government was no longer adequate to meet the needs of the town.

Warwick was, however, still an agricultural community with its tax base centered on land value. Warwick farmers, trying to retain the independence of an earlier period, were reluctant to concede that the town meeting form of government was no longer feasible. It was a difficult decision to make and only after the town was deeply imbedded in financial difficulties did the change to a city form of government, with a mayor and council, take place.

Harold P. Whyte, president of the Warwick Chamber of Commerce, was the force behind the successful movement to change the form of government first. Thanks to his determination, and after a number of unsuccessful attempts, the City Charter was accepted on April 21, 1931. The charter called for an election in November 1932, with the first mayor and city council to assume office in March 1933.

As 1932 wore on, Warwick was the scene of much political excitement. The *Warwick City Times*, under editor Arthur W. Paine, sponsored a lively "pick the Mayor" contest. The *Times*, which later became the *Warwick City Herald*, "due to legal complications," threw its support behind Pierce Brereton, who had been town solicitor from 1926 to 1932.

The 38-year-old Brereton was the great-grandson of Thomas J. Hill, the founder of Hillsgrove. In addition to attending Brown University, Yale University, and Harvard Law School, Brereton had served on the submarine chaser *Itasca 2nd* during World War I. Brereton was the front runner in the campaign and was elected mayor with little opposition. Warwick, true to its earlier political leanings, elected a predominantly Republican city council.

Seen here in a portrait by Karl Rittmann, Republican Pierce Brereton served as Warwick's first mayor. The popular town solicitor met with little opposition.

There were a number of interesting aspects as the campaign unfolded. Frederick G. Brown, Warwick Town Council president and a leader in the Republican Party, was challenged for a council seat by Nicola Zenga, a Potowomut businessman. Zenga's announcement, according to the Warwick newspaper, "was greeted with complete silence by the Republican leaders." Many Republicans feared that if they didn't nominate Zenga, who was very prominent in Italian-American circles, he might run as an Independent. If he did, he would draw not only the Italian vote but Democratic votes as well. Brown received the nomination, however, and was elected.

In 1932, Warwick was one of the few cities in the state to vote Republican, selecting Brereton and a predominately Republican city council. City Democrats were divided as many regulars had earlier favored Al Smith over Franklin D. Roosevelt. When Roosevelt clubs grew in Warwick, Democrats experienced inter-party quarrels. Warwick Neck's Peter G. Gerry, a Smith supporter, had conducted a losing campaign for the U.S. Senate. His defeat was blamed on his remarks against Italian-American Democrats. As a result of the defeat, he lost control of the party to Theodore Francis Green.

In 1932, on the national and state levels, the winning combination was F.D. Roosevelt for president, Theodore Francis Green for governor, and Robert E. Quinn for lieutenant governor. On November 7, 1932, the *Providence Journal* called the Green-Quinn victory "the greatest upset in history."

Even as Brereton assumed the position of Warwick's first mayor, the Democrats were gaining momentum. The Democratic Party in Warwick made the feisty John O'Brien their spokesman. Aided by the Green-Quinn victories on the state level, O'Brien mounted a campaign against Brereton and the Republican city council. O'Brien's campaign had all the energy and intensity that had marked the earlier campaign conducted by Patrick H. Quinn on behalf of the Democratic Party earlier in the century. As the depression worsened, a number of New Deal relief measures were enacted. Legislation was passed enabling Rhode Island to obtain federal funds for relief programs and to negotiate loans. As T.F. Green had been an early Roosevelt supporter, federal funds were dispersed through the governor's office and, in turn, Warwick Democrats benefited.

An attempt by Brereton and his Republican colleagues to fulfill their campaign promise to reduce taxes resulted in a further weakening of their party. They reduced the tax rate by .05 cents per thousand, but this was too little to please the voters and also necessitated reducing salaries of all city employees. Many city workers, who had previously been solid in support of the Republicans, now changed allegiance.

While Brereton was mayor, there were a number of changes that occurred on the state level that affected Warwick and altered its lifestyle. With the unemployment figures rising, more emphasis was placed on finding jobs for the needy and several projects were undertaken in Warwick. In March 1933, the State Board of Public Roads provided employment for 500 people at $15 per week. In Warwick, the director of Public Aid, Edward Godfrey, supervised the hiring of 250 workers, mostly unemployed mill workers and laborers who were heads of families, to work on the highway department. There were 658 applicants for the jobs, which consisted of three shifts of two days each, every week, for which the workers received a food order for $4.80. Godfrey also used funds appropriated for the relief of the "Outside Poor" to help families in great need.

During Prohibition, Warwick's shore line proved inviting to the bootleggers and smugglers. Carl Rettich's residence on Warwick Neck was locally known as the "Crime Castle" for its illegal activities.

In addition, organizations provided help for the more unfortunate. The Family Aid Society distributed milk to over 100 destitute families and the Red Cross distributed 7,500 bags of flour from November 1932 to April 1933 to 800 needy families. Also, a permanent clothing center was established at the Budlong Library building in Apponaug to provide clothes to those unable to purchase them.

During 1934, the number of employed workers in the textile industry dwindled from 34,000 in 1924 to 13,000. Mill owners claimed they were forced to cut wages and layoff workers. When they did, a strike resulted. The strike, called by the United Textile Union, began in the South and quickly made its way into Rhode Island. While Warwick's mill villages were not directly involved to the extent they were in the strike of 1922, many feared a repeat of the violence and the problems of the earlier dispute.

It was during the 1934 session of the General Assembly that a bill was passed, after a great deal of debate, authorizing a referendum for a racetrack in Rhode Island. The voters approved the racetrack by a 4 to 1 majority. It was also in 1934 that legislation was passed permitting the sale of hard liquor in clubs, saloons, and restaurants. Prohibition had ended in Rhode Island, if, as some critics observed, it had ever really existed at all.

Apparently, the voters approved of the first Green-Quinn administration for, in 1934, the Democrats swept in. Even normally Republican Warwick fell into the Democratic ranks, electing John A. O'Brien as mayor and four Independent-Democrats to the city council. Representative George Mills, Republican, of the Sixth Ward, voted with the four Independent-Democrats to give O'Brien the support he needed to name city officers. The Republicans, who continually had a majority of the old five-man town council, now found themselves with the inability to control the nine-man city council.

During O'Brien's term in office, he was not only mayor, but highway commissioner as well. This was a period when Warwick continued to have a "Sealer of Weights and Measures," "a Superintendent of Lights," and "a Tree Warden" as municipal officers.

O'Brien was instrumental in getting the General Assembly to pass an amendment to the Warwick City Charter that gave the mayor greater powers over the police and water boards. It abolished the old Board of Police Commissioners and created a Police Commission of five members, one of them to be the mayor and the other four to be picked by the mayor. The new Police Commission vested the authority of selecting the chief of police to Mayor O'Brien.

The Democratic mayor was met with great opposition from the Republicans on the city council, which was led by Frederick G. Brown, assistant treasurer of the Apponaug Company, and Albert P. Ruerat, councilman from Ward 1. Ruerat's political career began in 1933, when one of the Republican councilmen died and the party, anxious to find a young, successful businessman to fill the vacancy, asked Ruerat to run in a special election. Despite a growing Democratic swing in Warwick, Ruerat was elected and became a major adversary of Mayor O'Brien.

In 1936, while practically every area of the country saw Democrats sweep into office on the coattails of President Roosevelt, Warwick reversed the trend and put the Republican Ruerat in their highest office. It was, however, an extremely close election with charges of fraud and chicanery concerning the election ballots. Eventually, Ruerat appealed to the Superior Court to decide the results. He won the election by a scant 549 votes. Ruerat was successful in the next five elections and, in his sixth bid for the chief executive post in Warwick, he won by a plurality of 4,335 votes.

While most of Rhode Island voted Democratic during the New Deal era, Warwick continued to elect Republican Al Ruerat (back row, far right) as its mayor. (Courtesy Albert Ruerat Collection.)

During the 1930s, these members of Greenwood Volunteer Fire Company No. 1 maintained their building and apparatus at their station on Kernick Street. (Courtesy Greenwood Volunteer Fire Company Museum.)

When Ruerat was elected to office in 1936, Warwick was regarded by many as a "wide-open town." It was known more for its speakeasies, gangsters, gambling houses, and political chicanery than for its record as a well-administrated city. In one early election, a Ruerat opponent, pointing out the drawbacks of the farm- and resort-oriented city, said, "You can't even buy a suit of clothes in Warwick."

One of Ruerat's friends, upon hearing of his election, wrote, "we would be apt to commiserate rather than congratulate him upon his elevation to the stewardship of this corporate headache." Others noted that Warwick was an "economic catastrophe" and said Ruerat, "glided into the highest office Warwick can't afford." The mayor's annual salary at that time was $1,250, and the job was regarded as a "part-time" service. Ruerat, like his predecessors Brereton and O'Brien, was faced with the unenviable task of taking a number of mill villages, farms, and summer resorts and molding them into a city. Along with the political disorder, Warwick was faced with the devastating problems of the depression and the high unemployment rate in the city.

All was not "gloom and doom," however, for the need of inexpensive amusement and escape seemed more necessary than ever, and many saved their pennies throughout the winter for a summer's day at Warwick's amusement parks. Prices were cut drastically and a dollar went a long way. There was also a touch of luxury that could still be found, especially at the Warwick Country Club or Stender's Oakland Beach Yacht Club, where the more affluent where able to maintain their lifestyle.

The old silent movies were being replaced by the "talkies" and could be seen for as little as a dime. There were many areas in Warwick where dancing was featured and a number of bands competed for the biggest crowds. Nearly every church in Warwick had dinners, which often only cost 25¢ for adults and 10¢ for children. While some beaches charged a

10¢ admission and provided bathhouses and rafts, many areas were free and, as was the case at Gorton's Pond, an old automobile was used as a dressing room. In many of Warwick's communities, there was a sense of cooperation and friendship and churches played a large role in helping the destitute.

One of the major events, and one which changed Warwick immensely, was the building of a state airport within her boundaries. The impetus for an airport grew tremendously when an attractive young man of 24, Charles A. Lindbergh, took a $13,000 Ryan monoplane, *The Spirit of St. Louis*, from Roosevelt Field on Long Island, New York, to the Le Bourget Airport in Paris on May 20–21, 1927. This flight, made alone, over 3,600 miles across the Atlantic Ocean, made Lindbergh a national hero overnight.

Lindbergh's efforts resulted in the voters of Rhode Island approving a state airport by a vote of 76,281 to 9,369 in the general election of 1928. The main question was not "should we have an airport?" but "where should it be?" Early speculation and support placed it at Gaspee Point but, eventually, Hillsgrove was selected. This news caused a furor in the state with many demanding that the airport commission explain its action. The town council at Warwick quickly passed a resolution urging the selection of Gaspee Point rather than Hillsgrove. The Providence newspapers blatantly opposed the move, as did residents of Hillsgrove. In spite of the opposition, the commission, which had the power of condemnation, insisted that the airport would be at Hillsgrove and listed the land parcels that would be taken.

The location proved well suited to overcoming the disadvantages seen in the twenties. The great emphasis then had been on seaplanes and the fear that Hillsgrove would be difficult to spot from the air. As seaplanes gave way to land-based aircraft, sophisticated electronic devices made the necessity for visually prominent landmarks obsolete.

Rhode Islanders who had high hopes of seeing a modern airport emerge overnight were sadly disappointed. The state confined their effort in the early period to simply clearing and grading the field. During the early 1930s, the planes landed on grassy strips, as there were no paved runways. Private air companies erected their own hangars and it wasn't

When the original terminal building was constructed at T.F. Green Airport, Rhode Islanders came out by the thousands to attend the opening ceremonies.

until 1932 that the state began to build a terminal and administration building. When the State Airport was dedicated in 1931, it was the first state-owned airport in the United States. On September 27, 1931, two air shows at the newly dedicated facility drew a crowd of over 150,000. This was the largest crowd that had attended a public function up to that time. In January 1933, the state opened its administration and terminal building at 572 Occupastuxet Road.

By 1935, the state could boast of cement runways 3,000 feet long and 150 feet wide. A state report at that time pointed out that "These cement runways are the equivalent of 28 miles of a single-lane highway." In addition, the report stated, "there is a twofold drainage system, a double lighting system which illuminated the field at night to the satisfaction of night flyers."

With the necessity for accommodating larger and faster planes in the decades following its creation, the airport has grown to the extent that it dominates a large section of the city. From the late thirties to the present time, the forces pro and con have been battling to assess the proper status of the airport.

A major test for the relatively new City of Warwick came on September 21, 1938. This was the date of Rhode Island's most devastating hurricane. It left in its wake 262 deaths and caused an estimated damage of $100,000,000. With winds clocked in excess of 100 miles per hour and two tidal waves of almost 30 feet in height, it destroyed many waterfront homes and much of the amusement parks along the coast. Warwick, including Oakland Beach and Rocky Point, suffered the heaviest property damage of the state. Over 700 permanent residences and hundreds of summer homes in Warwick were totally destroyed.

The city had never before experienced such a violent act of nature and was not prepared. As late as 3 p.m. that day, the weather bureau was predicting winds of 40-45 miles per hour. By 3:30, torrents of rain poured down on Warwick and trees that had withstood the fury of a hundred storms began to topple. Mayor Albert Ruerat later recalled, "Up until the time the flagpole in front of City Hall came crashing down, we thought it was just another gale."

Before the Hurricane of 1938 did its damage to Warwick, Oakland Beach was one of the leading resorts in Rhode Island.

Not long after, Ruerat rushed to Providence to get his wife. He was fortunate enough to get her and return to Warwick. His description of the bizarre nature of the ride back to Warwick recalls the horror of the time. He said, "Freight cars were bobbing around like corks. Providence was under water. To avoid tree lined roads I had to drive on the lawns." When he reached Lakewood, Ruerat recalled, "There were no lights. I pulled into Everett Sprague's filling station. He had rigged up a gas motor for his pumps and filled my tank with gas." Ruerat chuckled over Sprague's wry comment, "We have a doozy of a storm."

After taking his wife to their home in Gaspee Plateau, Mayor Ruerat returned to City Hall, where he remained for the next ten days while Warwick reeled from the impact of the damage caused by the hurricane. Emergency stations were established in key areas and panic gripped City Hall when it was realized that hours had passed without any word from the Conimicut station.

Ruerat and an aide drove to Conimicut, barely escaping disaster as a section of the road at Buckeye Brook collapsed. Newspaper reports at the time noted that "the bay was a funnel, a wedge, a trap," as a tidal wave smashed into Warwick.

The *Providence Journal* book *The Great Hurricane* reported the following:

> Rocky Point, that Mecca of politicians and shore dinner consumers, fell like a house of cards before the southeast fury. The roller coaster was shattered, the great dining hall . . . was a soggy mass of lumber, a thousand bathing suits hung from the backwoods trees. . . . The oldest and most famous shore resort of the State was no more.

The hurricane's damage to Oakland Beach was so great that many totally abandoned any hope of saving their cottages. Many residents of the area, such as Father Valmore Savignac of St. Rita's Church and the Reverend Albert A. Gaisford of the Oakland Beach Union Church, will be long remembered for their work in rescuing people from the flooded areas and providing shelter for them. The National Guard was needed to help in the disaster, and Reverend Gaisford allowed them to use the church vestry as a billet. When the hurricane clouds cleared, there were 309 homes that had been demolished. The Oakland Beach Yacht Club, the waterfront roller-skating pavilion, and many other landmarks were gone forever.

The devastation in Conimicut was also great. Mayor Ruerat remembered, "Conimicut Point house was gone. There was nothing left on that part of the peninsula." The same tragic story could be told in nearly every section of Warwick. For ten days, most of the city had no power, no generators, and no telephone service.

The effects of the hurricane lasted for years and put an additional strain on the city's budget. By November 1938, six emergency WPA projects were in operation. They included repairs to bridges and culverts, repairs to Lockwood High School, and repairs to water mains. The pipes in the Buttonwoods section were left exposed when the water washed away the bank along Promenade Avenue, and the pipelines had to be lowered quickly before frost set in. Buckeye Brook was so cluttered with debris that it had to be cleaned in order to allow Warwick Pond to drain.

When Warwick began the long road to recovery after the Hurricane of 1938, it was obvious that the shore resorts would never be the same. Strangely enough, six monkeys which had escaped from Rocky Point in 1937 and were living in the woods on Warwick Neck not only lived through the winter, but managed to survive the hurricane as well, and were seen on the Neck and Spring Green Farm for at least another year.

Warwick was still trying to clean up the wreckage caused by the hurricane as she entered the decade of the 1940s. For a while, it seemed that even Warwick's oldest and largest amusement center, Rocky Point, had reached the end. The park was returned to its earlier owners, the Harringtons, as the entire area began to stagger back from the effects of the storm. The owners, however, never gave up hope.

In less than a year after the storm, plans were made to rebuild the park. In 1939, Thomas F. Wilson and a few others formed an organization that began building a great dining hall large enough to seat 3,500, and they restored the mechanical equipment of the huge covered swimming pool. When the project of restoration ran into difficulties, there was talk that the park would be divided into house lots. When this failed, representatives of the petroleum industry sought to use Rocky Point to locate its oil tanks. The Harringtons rejected this, as they feared it would be detrimental to the beauty of Warwick Neck and, instead, attempted to operate the park on a reduced scale in 1940–41.

Mainly due to restrictions placed upon them by World War II, the Harringtons were forced to curtail their activities and the park was not reopened to any great extent until 1945. At that time, it was sold to the Studley Land Company. In 1947, ownership passed to Rocky Point Inc., under the leadership of Frederick Hilton, Joseph Trillo, and Vincent Ferla. In 1949, Vincent was joined by his brother, Conrad, who remained with Rocky Point through a number of changes in ownership.

The outbreak of war in Europe pushed the everyday problems of the 1930s to the background as new crises arose. Prejudice and fear of the type Warwick witnessed with the Know-Nothing movement of the 1840s and the anti-Catholic, anti-black rallies of the Ku Klux Klan came to the fore. This time, it appeared as anti-German. In May 1940, when over 200 German-speaking persons gathered at the Norwood Hofbrau on Post Road, protests were heard. Residents of the area claimed, "They drank beer, sang German songs, gave the Nazi salute . . . and made anti-American speeches." Fortunately, the city administration refused to be panicked as Mayor Ruerat calmed irate citizens by promising to make a thorough investigation of the episode. No action was taken and, within a short time, the charges were forgotten.

In 1940, when the political arena was again filled with candidates, the Democratic Party split into two factions. Harold E. Flaherty and A. Norman LaSalle fought for the chairmanship of the party. When the Flaherty faction was outvoted, they refused to accept LaSalle and held their own meetings. The rift greatly aided the Republicans, who united under the leadership of their new chairman, Thomas Casey Greene.

During this time, rising costs and demands for improvements gave Warwick its first million-dollar budget ($1,064,119.50) on February 1, 1940. The tax rate remained at $22 per $1,000 valuation. Lockwood High School improvements and alterations were continued and a number of new Federal Works Progress Administration (WPA) projects

In the summer months, baseball was the number one sport in Warwick. This softball team was sponsored by Connie's Cafe in Apponaug. (Courtesy Bob Champagne Collection.)

were inaugurated. Major reforms in the organization of the fire and police departments were also undertaken at this time.

Warwick continued to be in the center of the political struggle in Rhode Island when William H. Vanderbilt took office as governor in 1939. Vanderbilt became very unpopular with certain elements in the Republican Party when he began to make major changes. Two of Vanderbilt's strongest supporters were Warwick's Mayor Albert Ruerat and GOP party chairman Thomas Casey Greene. They were criticized for this and were further challenged when the controversial Vanderbilt became involved in a wire-tapping scandal. An attempt within the party to oust Greene and Ruerat failed, and Ruerat once again was a candidate for mayor.

The Democrats in Warwick united after their split in a political duel between Robert E. Quinn and Walter O'Hara and once again selected John A. O'Brien as their standard bearer. With the threat of war in the background, Franklin D. Roosevelt ran for an unprecedented third term and easily defeated Republican Wendell Wilkie. In the gubernatorial election, Democrat J. Howard McGrath won a lopsided victory over Vanderbilt. Warwick, as in the past, bucked the Democratic tide and reelected Albert P. Ruerat. In this election, he trounced O'Brien by a vote of 8,313 to 4,671.

Within a very short period after the election of 1940, the city was facing a serious problem with the school system. As Warwick's population grew, there was an increasing demand for better schools. At that time, Warwick's cost per student was the lowest in the state. The state average was $97.75 and Warwick lagged far behind with $72.58. This low figure existed despite the fact that 41.2 percent of Warwick's budget went for the support of the schools. The system, led by Superintendent Warren A. Sherman, had 205 teachers, 20 grammar schools, and 3 secondary schools. Warwick's rapid growth brought the total number of pupils to 6,083 and the schools were overcrowded.

During the depression, Warwick was fortunate to receive federal assistance to enlarge and improve Lockwood High School, to build the Aldrich High School on Post Road in 1935, and the Samuel Gorton High School on Draper Avenue in 1939. City officials hoped that this aid and monies from the state and federal government to build a trade school would solve the problems of Warwick's school crisis.

In addition to the shortage of classroom space, the city faced an acute teacher shortage and dealt with serious discontent among the teachers in the system. Teachers' salaries in Warwick were very low and the actual amount of pay depended upon the sex of the teacher and the level of education taught. The range of salaries went from $900 per year for a female elementary teacher to $2,200 for men teaching at the senior high school level.

During this period, teachers became more vocal and began making their demands public. Led by John and Joseph McKeon, over 170 teachers, after a stormy two-hour session, rescinded the Warwick Teachers' Association's confidence vote in the School Committee that had been passed earlier. This was the beginning of an almost constant struggle over school issues in the city of Warwick.

In addition to the school crisis came the impact of the war in Europe and the threat to the United States. Early in 1941, city officials were called upon to preside at a very emotional program, when in January 1941, the first 35 draftees were inducted from Warwick and ordered to report to Fort Devens, Massachusetts.

The city was also faced with unprecedented pressures to prepare for any emergencies in the event of an enemy attack. Because the State Airport at Hillsgrove had become an Army

During World War II, the T.F. Green Airport was taken over by the U.S. Army Air Force. The public was invited to view the latest in military aircraft on "bond-rally" days. (Courtesy Albert Ruerat Collection.)

Air Field, and because of the close proximity of Quonset Air Base, Warwick felt especially threatened. Within a short time, 600 air raid wardens were appointed and special classes were held for auxiliary police.

Life in Warwick was altered abruptly when it was shocked by the news of the Japanese attack on Pearl Harbor on December 7, 1941. On the following day, President Franklin D. Roosevelt asked Congress to declare war on Japan. A dazed Warwick, preparing for war but not really believing it would happen, was now faced with a new set of problems as the outside world became important to the town. Warwick's young men and women, many of whom had never left the city, were now serving their country in Europe, Asia, and Africa. A new sense of awareness affected those both abroad and at home.

It was necessary to take a different view of the world and the city. An entire lexicon of new words came into everyone's vocabulary: Iwo Jima, 4-F, OPA, Blitzkrieg, lend-lease, Axis Powers, gas rationing, victory gardens, C.D., blackouts, war bonds, and, unfortunately, "gold star" mothers.

Some workers who had been long unemployed now found jobs plentiful. They pooled resources and gas rationing stamps to find transportation to work in the defense plants that quickly came to the area. A large number of Warwick residents found employment building "Liberty Ships" for Rheem's shipyard at Field's Point, which later became Walsh-Kaiser, while others worked at Quonset or Davisville.

The economic prosperity brought on by the war was often overshadowed by emotional pain and tragedy as Warwick's young men and women volunteered or were drafted for military duty. Nearly every family was affected, as over 4,000 men and women from the city served in the armed forces and were in every theater of the war.

The focus on helping with the war effort meant that Warwick would have to curtail many "normal" activities and abandon others. Building activity in the city slumped with the freezing of building supplies and the relatively high cost of construction. Warwick's free monthly rubbish collection system was also curtailed to save gasoline and manpower.

One of the projects abandoned completely concerned Warwick's tercentenary celebration. Plans included a number of gala events for 1942 and concentrated on the publication of a history of Warwick to be written by William Greene Roelker, president of the Rhode Island Historical Society. All plans were suspended, and the history was never written.

While Warwick's main interest from 1942 to 1945 was in the progress of the war and of the men and women in the armed forces, a great deal of time and energy had to be used in fighting adverse weather conditions. One of the major concerns was the limited supply of fuel and gasoline. Snowstorms in February 1943 brought additional problems and, by the middle of the month, bitter cold and a shortage of fuel caused the closing of the city's schools. Warwick physicians reported treating 24 cases of frostbite during that cold spell.

The perennial problems concerning increases in salaries for police, teachers, and city employees continued unabated and intensified as inflation quickly made fixed salaries inadequate. In addition, Warwick was faced with a new dilemma concerning the City Poor Farm at Buttonwoods. The problem took on new aspects when the State of Rhode Island passed a new public assistance law. By 1942, the old "poor farm" had but 15 inmates, with 10 of them eligible for old-age pensions. Editorials in 1942 termed the city farm "a costly and unsavory relic of an era that has passed." It was hoped that the farm, along with "victory gardens," could be used as a means of alleviating food shortages resulting from the war. In at least one instance, city workers left their regular jobs to help harvest the crops when farm machinery broke down. By 1944, the city disposed of all livestock and equipment at the farm after it was learned that the farm showed a net loss of $2,053.96 for the year.

The political struggle for power in the city continued with some modifications. In 1942, the Democrats selected Francis J. McCabe as their mayoral candidate. This popular figure had been postmaster of Apponaug during Woodrow Wilson's administration and had established the area's first real estate firm. The Republicans within the city had consolidated their power, and Albert Ruerat moved into an unprecedented fourth term. The only Democrat to win a council seat was Lambert M. Lind of the 8th Ward.

At 7 p.m., on August 14, 1945, President Harry S Truman announced the surrender of Japan, and World War II was over. The celebrations in Warwick, as well as in the rest of the state, were the greatest the city had ever experienced. Every church held religious services to give thanks for the end of the war. On September 21, 1945, Warwick's Civilian Defense officially came to an end. Over 3,000 residents served the organization during the war years and received recognition for their efforts. Plans were quickly made to honor the 4,618 men and women who served in the armed forces and for the 121 war dead.

During these early post-war years, Warwick continued to focus its attention on obtaining a suitable war memorial. In December 1946, the city's wartime wooden plaque in front of City Hall was taken down and a new, bronze, book-type honor role was created and placed in City Hall. In 1954, it was transferred to Warwick Veterans Memorial High School.

During the period following World War II, Warwick slowly emerged as a city rather than a group of villages. It was a period of phenomenal growth accompanied by both positive and negative factors. Led by William A. Grube, Warwick's businessmen started a local chamber of commerce using Gan's Hall in Apponaug as a meeting place. Road repairs and construction, both neglected during the war years, now became more necessary as automobiles began to come out of their wartime hibernation.

Changes in the police department also became imperative. Police Chief William C. Kindlen, after more than eight years in office, resigned to enter private industry and Deputy Chief Forrest R. Sprague became the new head of the police department. By this time, the police force was almost completely motorized, had a radio technician, and had adopted frequency modulation radio. When Sprague had first joined the force in 1930, officers walking the beat had to carry nickels with them in order to make a call from a public telephone to report to headquarters.

Of the utmost significance in the post-war period was the rapid inflation. Unprecedented rises in prices wreaked havoc with the city's economy and budget. Once the OPA restrictions were lifted, prices in restaurants and grocery stores rose as much as 100 percent. The days of the 5¢ ice-cream cone and the 5¢ cup of coffee were over. A pound of coffee went from 14.5¢ under OPA ceilings to 26.5¢ on the open market. In the grocery stores, hamburger prices rose from 28¢/lb., to 59¢/lb., and the cost of milk and

In the days before the "Big Mac" and the "Whopper," the Apponaug Diner at Williams' Corners took care of those hungry customers looking for good quality "fast foods." (Courtesy Bob Champagne Collection.)

milk products soared. In many instances, rents were increased up to 50 percent, and evictions were common.

This resulted in increased costs for almost all facets of the city's services and in a demand for higher salaries by municipal employees. In April 1947, Warwick's garbage collectors and incinerator operators went on strike over the pay loss and increased hours that resulted when they were transferred from the health department to the highway department pay scale. Mayor Ruerat agreed to reconsider the change and granted retroactive restoration of salaries to the earlier scale. After a one-day strike, the city employees returned to work.

Despite the fiscal problems and rising costs, Warwick continued to grow rapidly. Land was still relatively cheap in the city and taxes, while rising, were below those of other cities. For many, the American dream of the "little house with the white picket fence and garden" meant living in Warwick. Wage earners in the post-war period found Warwick's medium- and low-priced housing developments within their price range, especially with FHA mortgages and help from the federal government for veterans. As mortgages were fixed and wages increased, it became easier for families to own their own homes, and Warwick witnessed a building increase that turned it into a "bedroom community." After a wartime low of $225,258 for building permits in 1944, the post-war building boom saw the numbers soar to $2,614,771 in 1946 and $3,199,870 in 1947, surpassing the pre-war 1940 record of $2,031,968.

Because of its sprawling nature, many small-town characteristics prevailed, and as Warwick struggled to become a modern city, it found some areas reluctant to make changes. The Warwick Zoning Board of Review found it was busier than ever as requests

Village teams were very popular in post-war Warwick. Various village businesses supported teams such as this Conimicut football team in 1947–1948. (Courtesy Dorothy Andrews Collection.)

for changes and protests against change came in rapid-fire succession. Zoning Board meetings often attracted crowds in excess of 100.

Cowesett residents successfully blocked attempts to establish a post-war seaplane base at Folly Landing, while residents of Oakland Beach Annex tried in vain to stop Carl A. Berg from rebuilding a bathhouse and concession stand at Sandy Beach. The proposal by Pilgrim Land Developers to construct a complete "city within a city" on 145 acres of land, formerly known as the Massasoit Golf Club, brought about an unprecedented joint meeting of the city council, Zoning Board of Review, and the Planning Board, as Warwick tried desperately to grow in a logical manner.

In that same summer, Councilman George B. Salter was selected to serve on the newly created Kent County Water Authority and was made secretary to this very important agency, which was a step toward creating necessary facilities for a modern city.

Early in January 1948, Warwick faced a serious problem with a foul smog and horrible stench that emanated from the city dump on Sandy Lane. Despite repeated attempts to dynamite the site and drench it with water and literally tons of snow, residents of Oakland Beach, Shawomet, and Hoxsie suffered for many weeks before the problem was arrested.

Amid all the growing pains and serious problems, there were some light moments. On August 19, 1946, there was a wonderful time enjoyed by over 500 people when Warwick held its first full-scale block dance at Oakland Beach and, shortly after, its first soap box derby. In that same year, Buttonwoods celebrated Labor Day with a two-day holiday filled with festivities, and Conimicut sponsored sports activities ranging from a 5-mile "marathon" to an 18-foot crawl for babies.

Traffic to Warwick's seashore reached an all-time high as the beaches attracted over-capacity crowds. It was soon obvious that the bathhouses couldn't accommodate the numbers coming to the shore, and two motorcycle officers drew the impossible assignment of stopping the dressing and undressing in automobiles at the beaches at Nausauket, Buttonwoods, Oakland Beach, and Conimicut Point.

In the following year, Nausauket Beach held an "old-fashioned" Labor Day celebration starting with a "horribles parade" and ending with a clambake. Nearly every section of Warwick improved its recreational activities and more visitors decided to make Warwick their home.

The big news of the time was that Rocky Point was coming back to life. The 1938 hurricane had left 80 "abandoned and battered" acres in its wake and the amusement park hadn't functioned since that time, serving only as a summer camp. In 1948, shortly after Vincent Ferla, a Providence businessman, acquired the park, the amusement section was opened and many concessions moved in.

Rocky Point's opening on the first Sunday in June 1948 was the cause of a mammoth traffic jam, as over 35,000 patrons swarmed into the park. At 4 p.m., bumper-to-bumper traffic extended along Warwick Avenue to Cranston and the effects were felt as far north as Allens and New York Avenue in Providence.

At about the same time that plans were being made for the re-opening of the amusement park, a number of Warwick's leading citizens were engaged in working toward another project of far-reaching significance. This was the creation of the long-needed and hoped-for Kent County Hospital. The first step toward making this dream a reality came when Colonel Patrick Henry Quinn, dean of Kent County lawyers, donated over 8 acres of land on Tollgate Road for the site of the medical facility. Shortly after, Mayor Albert Ruerat launched a drive for an $800,000 building fund. Robert H. Champlin, one of Warwick's most successful businessmen and a philanthropist, started the campaign with a $25,000 donation. By 1951, the goal was reached when the hospital opened its doors for the first patients.

General View of Rocky Point, R. I.

This general view of Rocky Point shows the park at its prime before the Hurricane of 1938 wreaked its damage, causing the amusement center to remain closed during the early 1940s.

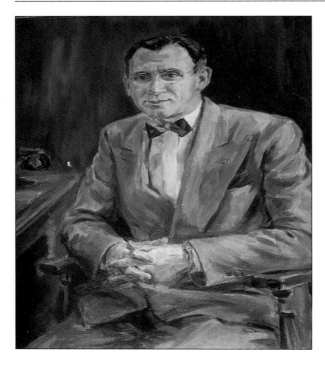

Seen here in a portrait by Karl Rittmann, maverick politician Joseph Mills successfully defied party leaders to win a stunning victory in the mayoral race in 1948.

During 1948, Warwick became the center of one of the decade's more exciting gubernatorial contests when Mayor Albert Ruerat decided to run for governor. The campaign began on a very optimistic note for the Republicans on the national, state, and local level. The National Republicans had bypassed Robert A. Taft, "Mr. Republican," in favor of the popular crusader Thomas E. Dewey. Early polls showed that Dewey was favored highly over President Harry S Truman and pollsters in Rhode Island felt the increased taxation and a sales tax would hurt Governor John O. Pastore and pave the way for a Republican victory.

Within Warwick, Republican Party leaders selected George Salter to succeed Ruerat as mayor. Local Republicans were visibly upset when Joseph Mills, Republican representative from Warwick's District 1 since 1938, challenged Republican leaders Thomas Casey Greene and Albert Ruerat by running for mayor. When Mills lost the primary, he turned Independent, rallied Democratic support, and challenged what he termed the "party machine and bosses." History reminds today's generations that the pollsters were wrong, as Truman defeated Dewey, John O. Pastore defeated Ruerat, and Joseph Mills beat George Salter by a vote of 7,881 to 7,335.

Within a few months of his inauguration, Mills was caught up in the difficulties caused by Warwick's phenomenal post-war growth. Mills, without a solid party foundation at this point, found himself in the midst of a series of factional disputes and broke with the Democratic Party chairman. The voters defeated his plea for a strong-mayor charter for the city. By the end of the decade, however, Mills was able to unite Independents, Democrats, and discontented Republicans in a drive toward the modernization of Warwick.

8. Warwick from 1950 to 2000

As technological, demographic, and economic changes came rapidly in the last half of the twentieth century, Warwick was in danger of losing her heritage and her beauty. The city was altered physically by the addition of large housing tracts where there once were farms, and by over 100 utilitarian type gas stations where there once were colonial dwellings. There was a great demand for more of everything, from schools to fast-food restaurants and from more roads to better bridges.

Television, while still in its infant stages, had become an integral part of many neighborhoods, as those with sets invited their neighbors to watch their favorite programs and the news. Warwick residents were more affected by the outside world than ever before. They watched in fascination and sometimes in horror as the United States entered the Korean War in 1950 and signed an armistice ending the war in 1953. They pondered the question of recognition of Communist China; the wonder of the Russian satellite, *Sputnik 1*; the Kefauver Committee against organized crime; the death sentence for the Rosenbergs, who had committed treason; and the bravery of Rosa Parks, the black lady who refused to give up her seat on the bus and brought about the beginning of the end of segregation on public vehicles.

In the rapidly growing city, Warwick residents could get free chest X-rays at the Chest-mobile to hopefully fight tuberculosis and cancer. Teenagers formed Elvis Presley fan clubs and clamored for a "drag strip," while senior citizens wanted a center for activities suited to them. In 1953, the *Warwick Beacon*, published by William Honig, became the city's local paper. By the end of the decade, Southern Rhode Island Publications assumed control of the paper. Warwick was thrilled when, in 1955, Burton "Buster" Bonoff opened the Warwick Musical Theater. There were 2,200 seats in the round tent and none were more than 20 rows from the stage. Throughout its existence, it attracted big-name actors and musicians. It was during the 1950–1960 decade when the police department began to use radar and a citywide permanent fire department was established.

There were mind-boggling problems of school department budgets, tax increases, the need for sewers, and better police and fire protection. Warwick also had to again deal with a major hurricane and found the airport at Hillsgrove was growing even faster than the city.

Population increases were responsible for forcing Warwick to change, as it was during this time that the city witnessed another massive wave of immigration. These newcomers came not from Europe or Canada, but from the older urban areas, especially Providence. The new residents, who were mostly second- and third-generation descendants of immigrants, sought the benefits of suburbia for themselves and their families. Unlike their ancestors who formed ethnic neighborhoods, the pattern of settlement in Warwick was based upon economic circumstances rather than language or religion. Most of the houses built in the fifties to accommodate the newcomers were built on speculation, and plats from 50 to 200 single-family dwellings seemed to mushroom throughout the city. Many were mass-produced houses of the Cape Cod, one-and-one-half–story, gable-roofed type or ranch-style houses. While there are a number of notable exceptions, many of the homes built in the fifties had relatively little architectural character.

The demand for more and better schools brought S. Wesley MacConnell and his associate, James Walker, to Warwick to build schools that would be functional and relatively inexpensive. MacConnell and Walker designs were well accepted, and the firm was responsible for all schools erected in Warwick from 1947 to 1958. This included Warwick Veterans Memorial High School, which had cost $3,000,000 and was filled to capacity when it opened in 1955.

The increased use of the automobile in suburban Warwick brought about the demand for shopping centers with large parking areas. In 1947, the Brown family opened the Governor Francis Shopping Center, the first of many in Warwick. This was followed in 1950 by the Gateway Shopping Center in Hoxsie. These shopping centers set the trend for the type of retailing that would develop over the next few years.

When the decade began, the Republican Party, eager to oust maverick Mayor Joseph Mills, selected the Republican state chairman Thomas Casey Greene, to run against him.

Warwick's attraction as an entertainment center soared when "Buster" Bonoff opened the Musical Theatre Tent in 1955. (Courtesy Henry A.L. Brown Collection.)

Mills managed to garner 8,257 votes to Greene's 7,710 and he remained in office. Two years later, however, popular Warwick state representative Darius Goff rallied young Republicans and rode the Eisenhower tide to victory. Among the new faces on the council in 1952 were those of Walter Richardson and Raymond Stone. Both became important political personalities later in the century.

While Goff was mayor, Warwick was struck with another devastating hurricane. On August 31, 1954, at 11:37 a.m., Hurricane Carol unleashed its fury on Rhode Island and, once again, Warwick suffered terribly. The barometer at Hillsgrove dipped to 28.79 and wind velocity was a sustained 90 m.p.h. with gusts up to 115 m.p.h.

Lucy Laventhol, writing for the fledgling *Warwick Beacon*, estimated the damage to Warwick at $3,000,000. She reported that the Oakland Beach and Conimicut Beach areas were hardest hit and said that 200 homes were devastated. At least 6 deaths of the 19 caused by the storm were from Warwick. Apponaug was devastated with flash floods, and cars at the Apponaug Company literally floated away. Houses at Arnold's Neck, Chepiwanoxet, and Potowomut were destroyed, as were boats and other vehicles. Rocky Point, so terribly devastated in 1938, was once again the scene of a great deal of damage and estimated its loss at around $250,000. In addition to the natural damage caused by the storm, there was looting of stores and homes. Mayor Goff requested martial law and, by nightfall, 200 National Guardsmen were patrolling in Oakland Beach, Conimicut, and Potowomut. On September 11, 1954, another hurricane, named Edna, hit the state but, fortunately, damage was kept at a minimum because the storm hit at ebb tide.

By November, the hurricane damage was cleared and Warwick once again turned to a lively political campaign. In this election, Mills, with a campaign slogan, "lower the boom on taxes," came back to defeat Goff by a vote of 12,473 to 10,197. For the first time in 22 years, the Democrats had a majority on the city council.

Warwick gained the spotlight early in 1955, when Mills refused to acknowledge the "lame duck" appointments made by the outgoing Republicans. He ignored the GOP police commission and zoning board and had the Democrats appoint their own. For a while, the city had two police commissions and two zoning boards. Mills and the Democrats took their fight to the Supreme Court and won on the police commission issue.

A major breakthrough in public services came when, in February 1956, Mayor Joseph Mills signed the necessary agreements to unite all seven of the city's firefighting units into one permanent fire department.

Joseph Mills was also known for his sociability and not only attended many weddings and testimonials, but he invited the entire city of Warwick to his daughter's wedding. The most exciting social function of his administration came in 1955, when he and the entire city entertained the Mayor of Warwick, England, Edward George Tibbitts, and his wife in a gala ten-day festival, the largest celebration in the city's history.

In 1956, the Democratic Party split into two warring factions, as Mills decided to withdraw from politics. This gave the Republicans the leading edge, and they backed Raymond Stone for the position of mayor. Once again, the big issue was the budget, which now exceeded $5 million with a tax rate of $27.50 per $1,000 valuation. Stone promised to hold the line and his opponent, John J. McCabe, stressed the necessity for sewers in Warwick. Stone swept in by a more than two-to-one margin. In this election, Warwick saw its first woman candidate for council, Mildred Anderson. She lost to Democrat Lambert Lind in Ward 8 by a 550 to 469 vote. Lind was the only Democrat on the nine-member council at this time.

It was now obvious that Warwick's residents were demanding services faster than the city could provide them. As early as the administration of John O'Brien, Warwick's second mayor, there was an attempt to bring in a strong-mayor plan of government to direct the growth of the city. Stone is usually given credit for increasing the power of the mayor and for encouraging city planning on a large scale. Mayor Goff had hired Stewart Pearson as city planner. While this was a move in the right direction, Stewart was given a very small staff. In 1956, Pearson was succeeded by his assistant, Glenn Kumakawa.

Almost immediately, in 1957, attention was focused on the police and fire departments. The police department at that time was in the basement of the city hall. There were three cells with constant water on the floor and many Warwick residents compared the jail unfavorably to a dungeon. The old two-platoon system (there were no police officers on duty from 4 to 7 a.m.) was replaced by a three-platoon system for around-the-clock patrols. James Lynch was appointed as chief, and the force was outfitted with new uniforms. Cars and all weapons were standardized, and a detective squad was added.

Financing the schools once again proved to be the city's biggest problem when voters, fearing a rise in taxes, turned down a bond issue for new schools. Mayor Stone found, however, that a limited bond could be listed without voter approval and he was successful in getting money to expand the schools at Cedar Hill, Warwick Neck, and Buttonwoods.

Warwick's first permanent fire department became a reality in 1956. Chief Thomas Duckworth (center) is flanked by Deputy Chief Harold Smith (right) and Deputy Chief Frank White (left). (Courtesy Greenwood Volunteer Fire Company Museum.)

By 1951, the Warwick Police Force had grown in both numbers and professionalism. Much of the success of the force is credited to Chief Forrest Sprague (first row, sixth from left). (Courtesy Michael Lynch Collection.)

To establish an industrial base, the Warwick Industrial Foundation was created. At first it selected the former Cole Farm for the site of the Pawtuxet Industrial Park. Later, the foundation erected a building on Jefferson Boulevard. Realizing that the need for sewers was one of the prime concerns, Warwick asked for money from the federal government to survey the area in Hillsgrove for that purpose.

As the decade closed, Warwick was getting an industrial base, its schools were attracting excellent teachers, a well-thought-out plan for zoning and growth was being developed, and the city finally had its own post office and postmark.

By 1960, Warwick had made the transition from an agricultural community to an important suburban area. During the next 30 years, Warwick changed from a suburban entity to a modern city of economic, industrial, and political significance.

When Warwick received a Home Rule Charter in 1960, a new era had begun. The charter paved the way for a much stronger mayor–city council form of government that had been advocated by former Mayors John O'Brien, Joseph Mills, and Raymond Stone. The old style, council-dominated form of government, with its emphasis on the parochial needs of the various villages, gave way to a much stronger central government that could better utilize existing city departments and create others as the needs of the city demanded.

Warwick's remarkable growth continued, as there were 68,508 residents, an increase of nearly 25,000 over 1950s number. Many of these new residents were of varied ethnic backgrounds and were predominantly Catholic in religion and Democratic in politics. Warwick, a Republican stronghold since the Civil War, became a Democratic city. The mayors for the next 30 years, Horace Hobbs, Philip Noel, Eugene McCaffrey, Joseph Walsh, Francis X. Flaherty, and Charles Donovan, were all elected as Democrats.

Republican Mayor Raymond Stone joins City Hall workers for cake and coffee in 1958. (Courtesy Mabel DelPonte Collection.)

All elections, however, were far from being rubberstamp-type party victories, but showed a definite trend on several occasions toward voting for the candidate rather than the party. During the last 30 years, Warwick has been home to a number of noted politicians of both parties who have achieved local, state, and national prominence.

One who achieved all three was John H. Chafee of Potowomut. Chafee's academic background and war record are impressive. He participated in the original landing on Guadalcanal in World War II and later served in the Korean campaign. In 1956, Chafee won a seat in the General Assembly as representative from District 3. In 1959, he became minority leader in the Rhode Island House of Representatives.

A number of political savants were taken by surprise when, in the 1962 gubernatorial race, Warwick's John H. Chafee defeated John Notte with a plurality of 398 votes. Chafee became the first governor from Warwick since William Sprague (the Elder) in 1838. From 1968 to 1972, Chafee served as secretary of the navy, and in 1976 was elected to the U.S. Senate, where he served until his death in 1999. He was then succeeded by his son, Lincoln Chafee, who was then mayor of Warwick.

During the 1960s, Warwick politicians were involved in some of the closest races in the history of the state. Another surprise of the sixties occurred in 1960, when Horace Hobbs was chosen by the Democrats to challenge Mayor Raymond Stone. The incumbent Stone was the strong favorite, as he had won the 1958 election by an impressive plurality. In 1960, Hobbs surprised everyone by beating Stone in one of the closest elections of modern times. Hobbs polled 15,391 votes to Stone's 15,216.

While the struggles in the political arena attracted a great deal of attention, Warwick was entering the modern age with significant accomplishments. In 1960, all of Warwick knew that Interstate Route 95 would go through the city and that Warwick would have a number of exit ramps from the new highway. This, of course, meant industry would be attracted to the Hillsgrove section of the city and, in 1960, Leesona moved onto Strawberry Field Road and Spiedel Corporation and the Mays Manufacturing Company moved into Hillsgrove.

This expansion of the industrial base, and the later growth of industry on Jefferson Boulevard, gave Warwick the expanded tax base she desperately needed. The years from 1964 to 1970 proved to be most significant years. Proposals for an east-west link connecting Warwick and Cranston (Route 37) became a reality in 1965. Route I-95 was connected to it that year and, shortly after, I-95 was linked to Jefferson Boulevard. This further aided the industrial expansion.

In 1964, finally after decades of debate, ground was broken for a 50-acre sewage treatment plant that was put into operation off Service Road in Hillsgrove in 1965. It was also in 1964 that bonds were approved to upgrade Warwick's waterfront areas and, very significantly, the Midland Mall became a reality. In 1965, Warwick took a big step forward in modern services with the building of a central library on Sandy Lane.

Further changes in Warwick's economic situation occurred when, in 1968, Sears opened the largest store in New England, with 180,000 square feet of space in the retail store and a 30-bay automotive center. Even then, plans were revealed for a 115-acre shopping center, the Warwick Mall. It would be the largest in Rhode Island and it was to be located

When Kent County Hospital opened in 1951, Warwick was providing its citizens with many of the modern services its growing population demanded. By the 1960s, the facilities could not keep up with the needs of expansion and growth. (Courtesy Henry A.L. Brown Collection.)

in the vicinity of the Midland Mall, now called the Rhode Island Mall. The Warwick Mall was completed in 1972, making Warwick the retail capital of the state.

By the mid-1960s, Warwick's retail sales soared to $68 million, an almost unbelievable figure when contrasted with the manner in which Warwick was derided in 1934, when a candidate for mayor sneered that Warwick was a "City where you couldn't even buy a suit of clothes." In 1964, after a great deal of deliberation, Sandy Lane was selected as the site for the new Warwick Central Library, another major step in giving Warwick services in keeping with its status as the second largest city in Rhode Island.

Much of the planning for Warwick's expansion came under the direction of city planner Glenn Kumakawa, who served under Mayors Mills, Stone, Hobbs, and Noel. While great strides in industrial and retail expansion were made under these mayors, Warwick also had to come to grips with a number of tragedies and problems. The horror of the assassinations of John F. Kennedy, Martin Luther King, and Robert Kennedy were brought into Warwick through the shrinking world of modern communication. On a local level, concern over the ever-increasing use of drugs and alcohol by Warwick's teenagers often appeared on the front pages of the newspapers.

The city dump continued to be a major problem and fires destroyed much of the old fabric of Warwick when the Apponaug Mill was almost totally destroyed by two devastating fires. The coming of jet-powered airplanes caused a great deal of concern about future plans of airport expansion. The population explosion of the era witnessed Kent County Hospital being forced to put patients in beds in the corridors, as the hospital couldn't seem to grow fast enough to meet the needs. Much of the same could be said of the schools, which seemed to be filled to the brim shortly after opening dedications.

As the 1960 decade ended with Neil Armstrong's walk on the moon in July 1969 and the reduction of American troops in Vietnam, world and national events helped make Warwick confident that she was ready to take her place as a modern Northeastern city.

Within a few years, however, disillusionment replaced optimism as new words such as Watergate (1972), legionnaires' disease (1976), Three-Mile Island (1978), and Ayatollah Khomeini (1979) shattered the dream of a beautiful future. For most Warwickites, the seventies meant a time of frustration over a sluggish economy, a growing dissatisfaction with politics, and a fear of involvement in the religious wars of Ireland and the Mid-East.

The school population in the city reached 19,914 to continue the problem of school financing. In addition to the threat of rising property taxes, Warwick residents worried when in 1971, Frank Licht, who had defeated Warwick's John H. Chafee for governor, announced the need for a state income tax and, on July 14 of that year, the proposed tax became law. Taxpayers and parents who were much concerned over school financing found that there was an even greater problem in the increased use of drugs by teenagers. Crimes related to drugs increased and this became the number one problem with which the police had to contend. When the age of majority was lowered to 18 years in 1972, police officials felt that the use of alcohol by "the younger group would result in more problems on the highways."

Despite the seriousness of the problems confronting them, Warwickites watched with wonder as old East Avenue, a small country road, became a major highway connecting

Warwick's reputation as a center of education was enhanced when the Community College of Rhode Island (then Rhode Island Junior College) built this structure on the Knight estate in 1972.

Route 5 and Bald Hill Road. Easy access to Route I-95 made that section of Warwick most desirable. It was because of this that the Rhode Island Junior College (CCRI) established its campus and built its $11-million multi-level, multi-purpose structure in 1972.

Democrat Philip Noel, running on the success of his administration as mayor of Warwick, defeated Herbert DeSimone by a 22,638 plurality and became the second governor from Warwick in a decade. Fellow Democrat Eugene J. McCaffrey conducted a very successful mayoral campaign in Warwick and easily defeated Republican Frederick J. Connell and Independent Joseph McKeon.

As Warwick moved forward and began to consider herself as an ideal community, the city was made painfully aware that there were large numbers of poor in the city and that discrimination against blacks was a harsh reality. Warwick has had a very small black population and as late as 1980, census figures reveal that there were only 409 blacks out of a population of 87,123 and in 1990, 673 out of 85,427. Dr. George Wiley brought the problem out into the open by saying that a black growing up in Warwick had no real identity. Wiley, a former Norwood resident and graduate of Aldrich High School, was speaking through personal experience. A chemistry professor at Syracuse University, he gave up his position to join the national staff of the Congress for Racial Equality (CORE), founded the National Welfare Rights organization, and spent his life attempting to get equal rights for blacks.

Both George and his brother, Alton, recalled the difficulty blacks had in buying a home in Warwick. They offered to pay the price asked for a house in Cowesett, but were turned away because of their color. When they finally did settle on a house in Norwood, neighbors circulated a petition to prevent the sale going through. When they finally purchased a home, they were given the "silent treatment," and it was not until much later that they felt at ease.

149

In 1973, Warwick was stunned when it learned that the Quonset Point Naval Airbase, after 33 years in Rhode Island, would close. Many Warwick residents were affected by this, and despite efforts by Secretary of the Navy John H. Chafee, Governor Noel, and U.S. Representative Tiernan, all of whom were from Warwick, the U.S. government closed its Quonset Base on June 28, 1974.

This loss of jobs at Quonset Base for many Warwick residents, coupled with a two-week teacher strike, brought about a great deal of trepidation. As in the twenties and thirties, Warwick again gained an unsavory reputation when it became known that "massage parlors" had opened at the Airport Plaza. Politicians, clergymen, and irate citizens were successful in bringing about the closing of these establishments. On the positive side, it was the first half of the seventies decade that saw the opening of the Boys Club in Norwood and the end of U.S. involvement in Vietnam, in which 20 Warwick men lost their lives. In 1974, Warwickites debated the pro and con of a state lottery, President Richard M. Nixon's involvement in Watergate, and the shortage of gasoline. Nixon resigned on August 8, "the LOT" was a popular success, and an odd-even system for gasoline kept the long lines from getting even longer.

In time, the political scene in Warwick brought few surprises. In 1974, Mayor McCaffrey easily defeated Byron Batty, and Governor Noel trounced James W. Nugent. Both Warwick politicians seemed invincible and yet, by the close of the decade, both were eliminated from the political arena. McCaffrey received the party endorsement in his bid for a seat in Congress, but was beaten by Edward P. Beard in the 1976 primary. Governor Noel, to the surprise of thousands, was defeated in his attempt to succeed John O. Pastore in the Senate when a relative newcomer to politics, Richard P. Lorber, defeated him in the

After many decades of trying to coordinate a number of small local libraries, Warwick built a large central library in 1964.

Democratic primary. In the election that followed, Republican John Chafee, a lifelong Warwick resident and former governor, went on to defeat Lorber. Senator John H. Chafee served in the U.S. Senate until his death in 1999.

Despite some economic fluctuations, Warwick was on its way toward financial stability in the seventies and made a number of great strides toward developing better recreational programs for Warwick's residents. An ice rink was started on Sandy Lane while Mayor Noel was in office. This rink was expanded during McCaffrey's tenure and a large, Olympic-sized, indoor pool was built. Buttonwoods Park was further developed and a bicycle path was added.

One of the most obvious steps into the modern age occurred when a police station was erected at 99 Veterans Memorial Drive. In 1975, Warwick had its first woman patrol officer, a preview of changes in the system that were to come. It was also the year that the T.F. Green Airport put in its first control tower and the *Warwick Beacon* became a semi-weekly publication. In addition, Warwick won praise with a handsome addition to the Warwick Central Library.

When the Metropolitan Life Insurance Company decided to build its New England regional headquarters at the old Jesse Dawley Farm off Bald Hill Road, the significance of Route I-95 and I-295 became even more pronounced as Warwick proved an ideal location for business offices as well as retail stores. Theater-goers had mixed feelings when, in 1976, the old Warwick Musical Theater tent decided on a hardtop roof.

In 1976, Joseph W. Walsh, an eight-year veteran in the General Assembly, became Warwick's tenth mayor. During his tenure (1977–1985), Warwick was faced with a serious deficit and a need to change the fiscal year. This was accomplished and, by the 1980s, Warwick was succeeding in extending its economic base as well as providing more services for its citizens.

Along with the celebrations of the bicentennial year, two of the most remembered events of the times were the loss of the America's Cup to Australia and the blizzard of 1978. While the loss of the cup was a traumatic event for many Rhode Islanders, it paled in comparison to the blizzard that hit the area on February 6, 1978. While the storm was forecast in advance, the state was caught unprepared for the rapid snowfall, which began in mid-morning. Eventually, 36 hours of snowfall blanketed the entire state with the worst winter storm of the twentieth century. At Green Airport, the official reading was 28.6 inches of snow, but it was much higher in other parts of the state.

When commuters tried an early mid-afternoon rush for home, chaos was the result. There was a 5-mile traffic jam on Route 95 and over 2,000 cars were abandoned. There were 21 deaths attributed to the storm and the area did not return to normal for several days. While the storm had its tragic consequences, it also brought about a great deal of cooperation and fellowship as neighbor helped neighbor to cope with the situation.

Once again in 1979, gas shortages were felt in Warwick, and even the mayor rode about on a moped until the situation improved. The school budget continued to soar and the issues of schools and sewers continued to be major areas of controversy in the city. Under Walsh, who initiated the idea of monthly gripe sessions at City Hall, citizens came to air their complaints on various issues ranging from airport expansion to school lunches. The sessions proved hectic but popular and his successors, Francis X. Flaherty,

Charles Donovan, Lincoln Chafee, Gerald Gibbons, and Scott Avedisian, have continued the policy.

The 1980s saw Warwick blending in with the rest of the state both politically and economically. The old Finast store on Post Road in Greenwood became Thomas McKeever's IGA and Joseph Walsh won his third term in a most impressive victory over Republican challenger A. Edward Norigian. Under the energetic leadership of Joseph Walsh and his successor, Francis X. Flaherty, more emphasis was placed on preserving Warwick's past while providing more recreational facilities and a positive business climate. Walsh, who had the ability to sense what the voters wanted, proved to be a popular mayor and served for eight years. It was during his administration that the city became very much aware of its heritage with the preservation and restoration of the beautiful City Hall and the publication of the Statewide Historical Preservation Report K-W-1 in 1981. The City Hall, built as the Town Hall in 1893 by William R. Walker & Sons, is an excellent example of Colonial Revival style and a striking visual reminder of Warwick's nineteenth-century heritage.

All of Warwick was shocked and saddened in September 1980 when it was learned that a bullet fired accidentally in Warwick police headquarters partially paralyzed teenaged police cadet Jimmy Langevin. The 16-year-old Langevin eventually went on to be one of the state's most illustrious politicians and is now serving in the U.S. Congress.

In 1984, Mayor Walsh made an unsuccessful bid to be the third Warwick politician to become governor of Rhode Island in the late twentieth century. While Warwick voted for Republicans Ronald Reagan, Claudine Schneider, and Edward DiPrete, they voted for Democrats in almost all other areas. Ward 6 councilman Francis X. Flaherty, in a Democratic primary that was one of the most colorful the city had ever witnessed, defeated Councilmen Joseph E. Gallucci and Joseph McGair. Stressing the need for controlling the economic development of the city, Flaherty went on to win with 76 percent of the vote.

During the late 1980s and early 1990s, Warwick continued to expand its industrial and retail base. Warwick's Bald Hill Road section developed very rapidly and the malls were attracting customers from all of Rhode Island and nearby states. Warwick's Route 2, "the golden mile," was acknowledged as the fastest growing retail district in the region. By the end of 1984, the $1.5 million renovation of the Council Chamber at City Hall was completed and opened to the public.

The year 1988 saw a number of changes in Warwick that indicated a bright future for many and sadness for others. The city received another A-1 financial rating, the Inn at the Crossing in Greenwood became a major Rhode Island hotel, and Conimicut Park was undergoing a transformation that changed it from a liability to an asset. In order to allow people to remain in possession of their homes in difficult times, an act was passed to defer taxes from qualified homeowners who met stringent requirements. Once the home was sold, the City would have first lien on the property and would recoup the taxes. Francis X. Flaherty won a third term with 71 percent of the vote. While the Republican Party looked hopelessly defeated, there was a bright side, as two promising politicians made their mark despite the Democratic landslide. Lincoln Chafee won in Ward 9 and young Scott Avedisian made a strong bid for a council seat in Ward 1.

The City of Warwick has become more diligent in saving and using its fine old buildings. In 1990, the old Buttonwoods School was renovated and became the nucleus for the Buttonwoods Senior Center. (Courtesy Gary Melino.)

Some of the longtime clerics were accepting retirement. In 1988, Howard Olsen, after 35 years as rector of St. Barnabas Episcopal Church, accepted mandatory retirement from the church. He continued, however, to work for the good of the community as he had for much of the late twentieth century. A few years later, in 1993, the Reverend Phanuel Bishop Covell Jr. completed his leadership at Warwick Central Baptist Church. Both men contributed to the ecumenical spirit in Warwick and enriched the community by their good works.

By the end of the decade, some of the bright shine of optimism was beginning to wear off as a number of the state's leading politicians, such as Joseph Bevilacqua and Vincent Cianci, proved to have "feet of clay." New fears of the eighties were the AIDS virus, the increased use of cocaine and "crack," the fear of a collapse of Social Security, and the enormity of the "trillion dollar" national budget. In 1989, the shocking news was revealed that teenager Craig Price murdered the Heaton family of Warwick. A saddened city soon learned that two years earlier, at age 13, Price had killed Rebecca Spencer.

By 1990, Warwick could boast of its accomplishments, as it was designated Rhode Island's "most fiscally healthy municipality," enjoying a $7.7 million surplus. Before the end of the year, however, the city was witnessing a series of problems. The economy was cooling off, there was a glut of condominiums, and the noise from the airport brought a series of complaints from irate citizens. There was also the fear that the reliance on computers might take away many jobs and that a computer breakdown might occur in the year 2000.

On October 19, a weak tornado touched down in Warwick with very strong winds. It started in Potowomut, crossed Greenwich Bay to Oakland Beach and Longmeadow, passing over Gorton Jr. High School. Fortunately, there were no injuries, but 8 homes suffered major damage and 13 had minor mishaps.

153

Seen here on St. Patrick's Day, 1992, at City Hall are, from left to right, former mayors Philip Noel, Raymond Stone, Horace Hobbs, Charles Donovan, and Joseph Walsh. (Courtesy Gary Melino.)

Some dissent in the Democratic Party was obvious and political savants predicted a political tornado in the offing. There was a primary battle for the mayoral seat when popular Mayor Francis X. Flaherty decided to run for governor. Both Charles J. Donovan and Michael Brophy vied for the position, with challenger Brophy nearly upsetting party-backed Donovan. In the struggle for power, Democrat Al Gemma bolted the party to run as an Independent.

Donovan won the primary and went on to win the three-way election in November. Donovan received 17,197 votes, Republican Lincoln Chafee 14,709, and Independent Al Gemma, 4,346. Donovan was the first non-lawyer mayor of Warwick since Horace Hobbs held that position. On the state level, Flaherty was defeated in the Democratic primary by Bruce Sundlin, who became governor when he beat Edward DiPrete for that office in the general election of 1990.

In 1991, all of Warwick and Rhode Island was devastated by the collapse of the credit unions and the obvious misuse of public and private funds by many trusted public servants. Over 45 credit unions and banks, some in Warwick, were closed by Governor Sundlin in an attempt to restore confidence and financial stability to the state. In 1991, financial and political scandals on the state level made Rhode Island the subject of ridicule.

On the brighter side, some of the fire and patriotism of earlier years made itself felt as Operation Desert Shield and Desert Storm witnessed the U.S. victory over Iraq and the liberation of Kuwait. Many of Warwick's citizens who were in the National Guard were called into service, and the cease-fire of February 28, 1991, was one of the happiest days in the city's memory.

In 1992, spirits in Warwick took an upswing as progress was seen in major physical projects that benefited Warwick citizens as well as the rest of the state. The Jamestown-Verrazzano Bridge was finally completed, women were gaining in politics and the professions, and the much-heralded Waterplace Park in Providence was well under way.

The political battle continued to heat up by the end of 1992. Michael Brophy received the Democratic endorsement for mayor and a stunned Charles Donovan decided not to enter the primary, but to run as an Independent in November. This election was one of the closest in Warwick's history, as Republican Lincoln Chafee led Michael Brophy by a mere 180 votes on election night. Eventually, with absentee ballots, Chafee won by 335 votes. It rivaled the election of 1960, when Horace Hobbs defeated Raymond Stone by a mere 147 votes.

By the year 1994, more political innovations were felt within the Democratic Party on both the state and the local level. Myrth York defeated Bruce Sundlin in the Democratic primary to become the first woman candidate for governor of Rhode Island. She was narrowly defeated by Republican Lincoln Almond in the November election. On the local level, two women, Carol Hagan McEntee and Gloria Kennedy, challenged Michael Brophy for the mayoral seat in the primary. Brophy won there, but was beaten in November by Lincoln Chafee, who received 56 percent of the vote and a clear victory. In that election, Warwick voters turned down a Home Rule Charter, passed a sewer bond referendum, and said "no" to casino gambling.

The T.F. Green Airport was making the headlines once again in 1996 with a $210 million expansion. The new terminal was completed and drew the admiration of passengers and officials alike. By the end of the year the airport was booming. Traffic was up 67 percent, due in large part to the inclusion of Southwest Airlines, a Dallas-based operation.

Lincoln Chafee ran successfully for a third term in 1996. He faced Democratic state representative George Zainyeh and Cool Moose candidate Timothy Rossano in a close race. In the next election, 1998, Chafee's popularity brought the Republicans to victory in the city. Chafee swept Warwick, taking all nine wards and getting 57 percent of the vote to Zainyeh's 40 percent. That election saw Democrat Gerald Gibbons trounce his opponent, David Watson, in Ward 2, enabling him to oust Carlo Pisaturo as council president. In that same year, Republican Scott Avedisian easily defeated Kenneth Smith in Ward 1. Neither politician realized that before the end of the century, they would be facing each other for the position of mayor.

By the end of the century, on October 24, 1999, the state was saddened by the death of Senator John H. Chafee. Governor Lincoln Almond appointed Lincoln Chafee to serve out his father's remaining 14-month term. The 46-year-old Warwick mayor was serving his fourth term when appointed. Gerald Gibbons, president of the Warwick City Council, became mayor in the interim period until a special election could be called in February 2000. This election again witnessed a heated primary battle in the Democratic Party and a great deal of dissension. Much to his surprise, Gibbons was challenged by a number of Democrats in the primary and the party was weakened and divided. Gibbons won the primary, but his party was seriously injured.

Mayor Scott Avedisian, former councilman from Ward 1, became Warwick's chief executive in the year 2000.

In that special election, the Republicans selected Scott Avedisian, who was in his fifth term as councilman from Ward 1. The race for mayor attracted five candidates and saw Avedisian winning an impressive victory as he gained 59 percent of the vote in contrast to Gibbon's 29 percent. A large crowd turned out for the inauguration of Mayor Avedisian, who took the oath of office at Pilgrim High School, his alma mater.

In the regular election in November 2000, the young mayor continued his momentum by trouncing Democratic candidate Michael Woods by a vote of 25,422 to 11,613. In that same election, former Warwick mayor Lincoln Chafee defeated Robert Weygand for the U.S. Senate, and Warwick resident James R. Langevin easily defeated his opponent, Robert G. Tingle, for U.S. Congress.

As the city of Warwick approaches the twenty-first century, it can look at its past with pride and its future with confidence. Statistics reveal that in the year 2000, Warwick, the state's second largest city, had a population of 85,808. With 35.5 square miles of land area, the city has a density of population of 2,417 inhabitants per square mile. The many homes are brought together with miles of streets and highways and are serviced by a modern sewer facility capable of handling 5,000,000 gallons of wastewater per day via 150 miles of collection sewer lines and 15 pumping stations. With nearly 19,000 residents under 18 years of age, Warwick schools play an important role in the city. Warwick has 26 schools with 869 teachers, and 12,138 pupils. In the last decade of the twentieth century, Warwick had a yearly school budget of approximately $72,390,657. During that decade, there were over 2,623 private firms in the city, which employed 39,341 workers and had a total payroll of $683,155,035.

These statistics, which are impressive when compared to those taken in 1931, when Warwick became a city, only indicate a small part of the story. What is not revealed is that Warwick, located near the geographical center of the state, is at "the crossroads of Rhode Island." The merging of Routes I-295 and I-95 in Warwick has meant that Warwick is at the hub of the modern interstate highway system. This has attracted much-needed industrial enterprise and has made Warwick the retailing capital of Rhode Island. In addition to its easy accessibility by truck and automobile, Warwick is well located on the main line of the Conrail Railroad and is a host city to the state's largest airport, which now boasts 164 flights daily. Both the malls and the airport have attracted large numbers to the city and fostered support and service industries, which have meant increased revenue for Warwick and its residents.

The early twenty-first century has seen some of these Warwick landmarks disappear. Two huge retail stores, Ann & Hope (December 2000) and Apex (January 2001) are closed, as are longtime grocery stores such as Almacs and Star. Throughout the nineteenth and twentieth centuries, Warwick has been a playground for the state as its 39 miles of coastline have fostered shore resorts and amusement parks. This has also changed. Rocky Point, long the Mecca for youngsters of all ages in the summer, closed to the public in 1995; Sholes Skating Rink made way for a new hotel in 1999; and the Warwick Musical Theater has been demolished.

In its wake, however, new hotels, restaurants, and parks have been built. Goddard Memorial State Park and the city's parks and beaches at Conimicut, Buttonwoods, and Oakland Beach are experiencing revitalization and a new popularity. The Warwick Museum, the Mickey Stevens Sports Complex, and excellent Senior Centers, along with very modern and efficient police, fire, and sanitation departments, are all assets that make Warwick a pleasant place in which to live. The city administration, especially since World War II, has steadily sought better planning, zoning, and efficiency in government. Warwick's central location in Rhode Island, the easy access to modern highways, the excellent state airport, and the planned railway improvements make the city easily accessible from all areas of the United States.

The result is that Warwick, "the City at the Crossroads," is a prime area for further industrial, commercial, and population growth. Fortunately, through its concerned citizens, Warwick is proud of its heritage and is working to maintain the balance between a proud past and a bright future.

While Warwick is Rhode Island's second largest city, it still maintains its suburban character. There is no single "downtown." However, Apponaug, with its city hall, post office, churches, and small businesses, serves as downtown.

157

BIBLIOGRAPHY

Arnold, Samuel G. *History of the State of Rhode Island and Providence Plantations*. 2 vols. New York: Dean Appelton & Co., 1860.

Bartlett, John Russell, ed. *Rhode Island Colonial Records*. 10 vols. Providence: Knowles, Anthony & Co., 1856–1865.

Beers, J.H. & Co. *Representative Men and Old Families*. 1908.

Belcher, Horace. "Collection of Letters and Articles." 1885–1952.

Brayton, Gladys W. *Other Ways and Other Days*. East Providence: Globe Printing Co., 1976.

Buckley, Abby. *Chad Brown Memorial*. New York: Brooklyn Daily Eagle Press, 1888.

Carroll, Charles. *Rhode Island: Three Centuries of Democracy*. 4 vols. New York: Lewis Historical Publishing Co., Inc., 1932.

Clauson, J. Earl. *These Plantations*. Providence: Roger Williams Press, 1937.

Chidsey, Donald B. *The American Privateers*. New York: Dodd, Mean & Co., 1962.

Coleman, Peter S. *The Transformation of Rhode Island, 1790–1860*. Providence: Brown University Press, 1969.

Conley, Patrick. *Rhode Island Album*. Norfolk, VA: Donning Co. Publishers, 1986.

Cowell, Benjamin. *The Spirit of '76 in Rhode Island*. Boston: A.J. Wright, Printers, 1850.

Davis and Robinson. *A History You Can See*. Providence: Rhode Island Publications Society, 1986.

Davis, Hadassah. *What Cheer, Netop*. Providence: Rhode Island Publications Society, 1986.

Department of the Secretary of State. *R.I. Manual*. Greenfield: T. Mowry & Sons, 1917.

Downing, Antoinette F. *Early Homes of Rhode Island*. Richmond, VA: Garrett & Massie, Inc., 1937.

Field, Edward. *Revolutionary Defences of Rhode Island*. Providence, 1886.

———. *The State of R.I. and Providence Plantations*. 3 vols. Boston: Mason Publishing Co., 1902.

Fowler, William S. "Report of the Narragansett Archaeological Society." October 1952 and October 1956.

Fuller, Oliver Payson. *The History of Warwick, Rhode Island*. Providence: Angell, Burlingame & Co., 1875.

Gorton, Samuel. *Simplicities Defence*. London, 1646. Reprinted, 1835.

Greene, Welcome Arnold. *The Providence Plantations*. Providence: J.A. & R.A. Reid, Publishers, 1886.

Great Hurricane and Tidal Wave. *Providence Journal*, 1938.

"Harris Papers." Rhode Island Historical Society Collections, Vol. X. Providence, 1902.

Hedges, James B. *The Browns of Providence Plantations*. 2 vols. Cambridge, MA: Harvard University Press, 1952 and 1958.

Leach, Douglas E. *Flintlock and Tomahawk*. New York: W.W. Norton & Co., 1958.

Leach, Douglas E. *King Philip's War*. Providence: Rhode Island Historical Society, 1963.

Lippincott, Bertram. *Indians, Privateers, and High Society*. New York: J.B. Lippincott, 1961.

Longo, Mildred Santille. *Picture Postcard Views of Rhode Island Lighthouses and Beacons*. Providence: Rhode Island Publications Society, 1990.

Malloy, Scott. *Streetcar Employees, Division 618*. 1977.

Mayor, Dorothy. "I Remember Apponaug." Warwick Museum, 1981.

McLoughlin, William G. *Rhode Island: A History*. New York: W.W. Norton & Co., 1978.

McPartland, Martha R. *History of East Greenwich 1677–1960*. East Greenwich: East Greenwich Free Library Association, 1960.

Mohr, Ralph S. *R.I. Governors for 300 Years*. Providence: Oxford Press, 1959.

Rhode Island Historical Preservation Commission Reports Statewide. 1980–1993.

Rider, Hope S. *Valour Fore & Aft*. Annapolis, MD: Naval Institute Press, 1977.

Showman, Richard K., ed. *The Papers of General Nathanael Greene*. 6 vols Chapel Hill, University of North Carolina Press, 1976–1990.

Simister, Florence. *The First 100 Years (Hospital Trust) Rhode Island Hospital Trust*. Providence, 1967.

Smith, Hedley. *Gift of Armor*. New York: Vantage Press, 1968.

Steffens, Lincoln. "Rhode Island: A State for Sale." *McClure's Magazine*. No. 4. February 1905.

Steinberg & McGuigan. *R.I.: An Historical Guide*. Providence: Rhode Island Bicentennial Foundation, 1976.

Taft, Lewis. *Profile of Old New England*. New York: Dodd, Mead & Co., 1965.

Walker, Anthony. *So Few the Brave*. Newport: Seafield Press, 1981.

Williams, Roger. *A Key into the Language of America*. London, 1643; Reprinted: Providence, 1936.

Woodward, Carl R. *Plantation in Yankeeland*. Chester, CT: Pequot Press, 1971.

WPA Writers Project. *Rhode Island: A Guide to the Smallest State*. Boston: Houghton-Mifflin, 1937.

Wright, Marion, and R.J. Sullivan. *The R.I. Atlas*. Providence: Rhode Island Publications Society, 1982.

The colorful, and often controversial, Police Chief Ellis Cranston led this parade on April 28, 1918. His department was very small and was located in the basement of Town Hall. (Courtesy Dorothy Mayor Collection.)

INDEX